पारिजात-हरण

Kṛṣṇa Steals the Pārijāta

edited by

Harsha V. Dehejia

DK PRINTWORLD

Cataloging in Publication Data — DK
[Courtesy: D.K. Agencies (P) Ltd. <docinfo@dkagencies.com>]

Pārijāta-haraṇa = Kr̥ṣṇa steals the pārijāta / edited by
Harsha V. Dehejia.
pages cm
English and Hindi.
ISBN 13: 9788124608043

1. Krishna (Hindu deity). 2. Krishna (Hindu deity) — Art.
3. Trees — Religious aspects — Hinduism. I. Dehejia, Harsha
V., editor. II. Title: Kr̥ṣṇa steals the pārijāta.

DDC 294.52113 23

ISBN: 13: 978-81-246-0804-3
First published in India in 2015

Front cover, Bundi, 18th Century,
Dehejia Collection of Krishna Art.
Back cover, painting by Shri Girish Patel

Designed by Paul Crupi, Ottawa, ON, Canada

Printed and published by:
D.K. Printworld (P) Ltd.
Regd. Office : 'Vedaśrī', F-395, Sudarshan Park
(Metro Station: Ramesh Nagar), New Delhi - 110 015
Phones : (011) 2545 3975; 2546 6019; Fax : (011) 2546 5926
e-mail : indology@dkprintworld.com
Web : www.dkprintworld.com

Contributors

Narmada Prasad Upadhyaya, a member of the Commercial Tax Appellate Board in Bhopal, has written extensively on Indian Art. Among his books are *Bharatiya Chitrankan Parampara*, *The Concept of Portrait*, *Kanheri Gita Govinda*, *Paar Roop Ke*, and *Colour's Fragrance*. He is currently working on the art and culture of Bundelkhand. He was given the Kala Bhushan Award in 2003.

Dr. Mahendra Kumar Mishra is a litterateur from Odisha, India. He has authored *Oral Epics of Kalahandi*, *Visioning Folklore: Critical Essays on Western Odisha*, and *Folk Tales from Odisha*. He is the recipient of Sahitya Academy Award for his cultural analysis of folk literature of Odisha. Dr Mishra has also received the Veer Shankar Shah Raghunath Shah Award from the Government of Madhya Pradesh for his lifetime contribution in tribal culture and literature in India.

Christopher Austin is Professor of Religions Studies in the Department of Classics, Dalhousie University, Halifax, Nova Scotia, Canada. He has written extensively on Puranic subjects including *Parijat Haran*. This work was funded by the Social Sciences and Humanities Research Council of Canada.

Vijay Sharma is an artist specializing in Pahāṛī miniature paintings. He was awarded the Padma Shri by the Government of India and an Honorary Doctorate by Himachal University. He has written many books and articles on Pahāṛī Art.

Harsha V. Dehejia is Professor of Indian Studies in the College of Humanities, Carleton University, Ottawa, ON, Canada. His main interest is in Indian Aesthetics. He has many books to his credit, had made a documentary film and has curated many exhibitions.

Painting by Vijay Sharma

The Pārijātaharaṇa in Mahābhārata and Harivaṁśa

Christopher R. Austin

The narrative and artistic traditions of the Pārijātaharaṇa appear to find their basis in the great epic *Mahābhārata* (*Mbh*) and its supplement *Harivaṁśa* (*HV*). Together these texts provide the earliest extant Sanskrit sources of this episode of Kṛṣṇa's life. From approximately the fifth century onwards, one then finds many elaborations of this tale in the Purāṇas, Kāvya or courtly poetic literature, artistic representations and vernacular retellings. *HV*'s appendix I.29, a later addition to the early critical form of the *HV* text, constitutes perhaps the most important articulation of the episode in the written Sanskrit tradition.

In the critical text of *Mbh*, the story of the theft of the tree is never related, and one finds only two short, passing references to the deed. One finds references in *Mbh* to the *pārijāta* simply as a species of tree (3.155.46, 9.36.60, 11.11.19). The first of these occurs in the context of book 5, where the Pāṇḍavas' uncle Vidura warns the evil Duryodhana against acting on a foolish plan to kidnap Kṛṣṇa and as a warning against the doomed plot Vidura enumerates a number of Kṛṣṇa's heroic feats which bespeak his incredible strength, and among these is the Pārijātaharaṇa (5.128.48):

> King Varuṇa was conquered by [Kṛṣṇa] of limitless energy, and Pāvaka [Agni], and [Indra] the husband of Śacī was publicly defeated by [Kṛṣṇa] who removed the *pārijāta*.

The second reference to this event is in book 7, where Dhṛtarāṣṭra, grieving over the likelihood of his sons' destruction at the hands of the mighty Kṛṣṇa, also recounts some of the deeds which bespeak Kṛṣṇa's invincibility (7.10.22-23):

> [Kṛṣṇa] the hero, having mounted upon [Garuḍa] Vainateya and terrified [Indra's heavenly city] Amarāvatī, removed the *pārijāta* from the home of Mahendra [Indra]. And Śakra [Indra] forgave that [deed], knowing [Kṛṣṇa's] power. Who has heard of anyone unconquered by Kṛṣṇa, even among kings?

It was precisely in order to elaborate upon such references that the poets of *HV* developed their Kṛṣṇacarita attached to *Mbh*. It is in this context of *HV adhyāyas* 91-92, where Kṛṣṇa acquires many wives and riches, that the *pārijāta* episode is related in full.

In *adhyāya* 91, Kṛṣṇa goes to war against the great demon Naraka (Bhauma), who has seized the wealth of the gods, kidnapped 16,100 women and taken possession as well of the earrings of Aditi (mother of the gods), and of Varuṇa's umbrella. Kṛṣṇa advances to Naraka's city Prāgjyotiṣa, where he wages war against Naraka and his army, mounted upon his majestic eagle Garuḍa and accompanied by Satyabhāmā. Kṛṣṇa slays Naraka with his *cakra*, takes the hoards of riches and has them sent back to Dvārakā, and rescues the 16,100 women. In order to return Aditi's earrings and the gold-producing umbrella of Varuṇa, Kr̥ṣṇa flies up to heaven on Garuḍa, accompanied by Satya-bhāmā. After Kr̥ṣṇa has delivered the earrings and umbrella and received the courteous hospitality and blessings of Indra, Indra's wife Śacī and Aditi, he and Satyabhāmā are left free to wander through Indra's heaven as they please. Here (92.62-70) is where we find the critical text *HV*'s Pārijātaharaṇa episode, properly speaking:

> Having mounted Vainateya [Garuḍa] together with Satyabhāmā, strolling about the pleasure-grounds of the gods and being reverenced by them, the great-armed one saw the great *pārijāta* tree, a divine and celebrated *caitya* [tree], in a pleasure-park of Vasava. [This] divine [tree] was always in bloom and possessed the most wonderful pure perfume. Every person who approached it remembered his former birth. Viṣṇu, whose valour is unbounded, having forcibly pulled up that great tree under protection by the gods, raised it up. Hari looked upon Satyabhāmā the divine *apsaras*, then went forth to Dvāravatī on a wind-swept path. [Indra] the great-armed king of gods, hearing about that deed of Kr̥ṣṇa, approved of it and said "The deed is done". Kr̥ṣṇa Arindama, being praised by the thirty [gods] and lauded by the troops of great sages, proceeded to Dvārakā from the world of the *devas*. The great-armed one, having flown across a long path as though it were a small one, honoured by the king of gods, saw the city of Yādavas. The Blessed Lord Vasavanuja Viṣṇu, with Garuḍa as his mount, having done the great deed, came [back] to Dvārakā.

In *HV* account, Kr̥ṣṇa does not fight with Indra over the tree as he does so in other more popular renderings, and in fact Indra's response is approval (*anumene*) and resignation (*kr̥tam karma*). Second, while Satyabhāmā is present here, she plays almost no role whatsoever, except that Kr̥ṣṇa somewhat mysteriously looks at her when he uproots the tree. Kr̥ṣṇa rather seems to desire it purely as an object of wealth with which he could beautify the city of Dvārakā.

In *HV* 94.19-23, some details are provided about the tree itself. Most notable is that, by its special powers, people in its proximity may perceive each others' immortal souls within their mortal bodies (*te 'nyonya dad śur . . . dehabandhān amānu ān,* 94.20). While the mountain-peak Maṇiparvata is placed down in the women's quarters (94.22), the tree is said only to be located in a pleasant spot (*arcyam arcitam avyagram i e deśe nyaveśayat).*

What is perhaps most striking about these critical text references is their apparent disagreement over whether or not Kr̥ṣṇa battled with Indra for possession of the tree. In the actual narrative at *HV* 92.62-70, the tree is removed without conflict and indeed the act is approved by Indra. *Mbh* verses 7.10.22-23 seem to corroborate this non-confrontational account, specifying as well that Indra forgave or disregarded the tree's removal (*mar itavān*) knowing better than to fight with the powerful Kṛṣṇa. And yet other critical text references speak of conflict with the gods over its removal (*HV* 93.58) or more commonly of conflict with Indra (*Mbh* 5.128.48; *HV* 105.10; 109.42-45). *HV* 97.14 meanwhile suggests that Kṛṣṇa had no fear of Indra (*acintayitvā devendra)* but this does not state either way whether they fought or not.

Clearly it is too simplistic to contrast *Mbh* and *HV* critical texts with later versions. The narrative tension is rather ironed out by the later *HV* poets themselves who, in inserting additional material into the text, made things absolutely clear that Kṛṣṇa did fight an epic battle with Indra for possession of the tree, and he did it to appease his sulking and jealous wife Satyabhāmā. The Bhandarkar critical text of *HV* reconstructs for us the oldest version of the poem available, dating to roughly second-third centuries CE. As this poem was then passed down all over India across the generations, additions were made to the poem, and these additions are available to us now in *HV* appendices of the Bhandarkar edition. It is here in these appendices that we find the later generations of *HV* scribes developing further portions of the poem which they felt needed enhancing, and the Pārijātaharaṇa is one of the most significantly reworked sections of the entire *HV*. We turn now to Appendix I.29 and to the factors prompting its incorporation into *HV*.

The Pārijātaharaṇa in Harivaṁśa Appendix I.29

The set of *HV* appendices I.29-29F is interposed between the critical text of *HV adhyāyas* 92 and 93, which describes the city of Dvārakā or Dvāravatī. Almost all *HV* manuscripts in India contain this material, and so it is impossible to know where precisely they may have originated from. Popular and widespread as they are, it is clear that these chapters are not part of the original text, for they are absent from the "keystone" manuscripts Ś1, Ñ1 and M1-3. The Appendix I.29-29F block of material likely did not get incorporated into the various *HV* manuscript copies across India until at least the eleventh century CE. These seven appendices treat the Pārijātaharaṇa (29), the *puṇyaka* vow and other womens' *vratas* (29A), the story of the demon Nikumbha (29B), Śiva's *pārijāta* grove and the attack made upon it by the demon Andhaka (29C), an account of a seaside picnic enjoyed by Kṛṣṇa and the Vṛṣṇis (29D), the abduction of Kṛṣṇa's granddaughter Bhānumatī (29E), and the substantial tale of Pradyumna and the demon princess Prabhāvatī (29F).

Our concern here is solely with the first of these seven appendices, which corresponds to chapter II (*Viṣṇuparvan*) 65-76 of the older "Vulgate" edition *HV* (Kinjawadekar 1936) containing the commentary of Nīlakaṇṭha, and which I will refer to simply as Appendix 29. Although it does not form part of the critical *HV* text, it constitutes perhaps the most important and popular source of Parijātaharaṇa in the Sanskrit textual tradition. Here however it will suffice to outline the content of Appendix 29, and to ask how and why this elaboration was appended to the critical *HV*'s short account.

Although in the critical text *HV* at the conclusion of *adhyāya* 92 Kr̥ṣṇa has already returned to Dvārakā with the tree, Appendix 29 retells the entire tale anew, in a sense ignoring the short critical text episode of the tree's theft. This version is nearly 800 verses and so I shall only summarize it here rather than translate it in full.

Appendix 29 begins with the appearance of the sage Nārada, who arrives in Dvārakā to find that Rukmiṇī has just completed a fast at Mount Raivataka. Nārada brings with him a flower of the miraculous *pārijāta* tree and describes its many supernatural qualities. At Nārada's prompting, Kr̥ṣṇa gives the flower to his chief and eldest wife Rukmiṇī who is thereby distinguished as his favourite wife. Satyabhāmā, Kr̥ṣṇa's younger and somewhat more volatile wife, learns of this and flies into a jealous rage, sulking in her private chambers. The poet here treats her in the classical Kāvya style with a description of her feminine charms and of her endearing tantrum. Naturally Kr̥ṣṇa comes to visit and to inquire why she is upset. The source of Satyabhāmā's jealousy, the gift of the single *pārijāta* flower to Rukmiṇī is soon identified, and Satyabhāmā proposes that Kr̥ṣṇa to make up for this insult to her, obtain for her the entire *pārijāta* tree. Here Nārada appears to explain the genesis of the tree. While in much Hindu mythology, the *pārijāta* tree is usually thought to have been produced at the churning of the ocean (e.g. *Viṣṇu Purāṇa* 1.9.93), a different origin is explained here: this tree was created in heaven by Kaśyapa for his wife Aditi, the mother of the gods, so that she could carry out certain rituals to enhance her auspiciousness and beauty. Thus we now begin to see that, beyond the initial matter of Satyabhāmā's jealousy, this tree has a special significance for women as a ritual object and bestower of *saubhāgya* (marital felicity) and other qualities desired by married women. Over the course of Appendices 29 and 29A, this aspect of the tree — its ritual significance and usage in womens' *vratas* (ritual vows) to ensure beauty, the birth of sons and the long life of their husbands — becomes increasingly emphasized, and Satyabhāmā's jealousy and desire for the tree consequently takes on a greater religious significance.

Kr̥ṣṇa's first attempts to acquire the tree are civil and diplomatic, but doomed to failure. He dispatches a reluctant and pessimistic Nārada to act as negotiator and to appeal to Indra for the tree. But as Nārada knows all too well, Indra will not part with the *pārijāta* under any circumstances, and his travels back and forth from Dvārakā to heaven come to naught. Kr̥ṣṇa decides to seize the tree by force. Kr̥ṣṇa mounts Garuḍa accompanied by Sātyaki (here Satyabhāmā does not accompany Kr̥ṣṇa as in many popular representations), and his son Pradyumna takes flight along with him in a sky-going chariot. Kr̥ṣṇa quickly arrives in heaven, seizes the tree, and the great battle begins. Indra, mounted on Airāvata and accompanied by his son Jayanta squares off against Kr̥ṣṇa, mounted upon Garuḍa and accompanied by his son Pradyumna. Indra is also assisted by a warrior named Pravara, who is resisted by Sātyaki. Various skirmishes between the opposing figures are described, but by the end of the day the conflict is unresolved, and the combatants retire. Kr̥ṣṇa, Pradyumna and Sātyaki, still in possession of the tree, visit a mountain called Pāriyātra in the Western Vindhya range, and there Kr̥ṣṇa worships a form of Śiva called Bilvodakeśvara.

The next day, Indra and Kr̥ṣṇa resume their fight, and now it is so fierce that the entire universe trembles. Finally the mother and father of the gods, Aditi and Kaśyapa, call a halt to the quarrelling: Aditi tells Indra that he must part temporarily with the *pārijāta* tree so that Satyabhāmā can perform a vow with it called the *puṇyaka*; thereafter it will be taken back to heaven. Kr̥ṣṇa returns in triumph to Dvārakā where all are amazed by the miraculous tree, and where Satyabhāmā prepares to carry out the *puṇyaka* vow. Nārada is required as a third party for this ritual, and so he is summoned and received with all due hospitality. The *puṇyaka* vow requires that Kr̥ṣṇa be tied to the *pārijāta* tree and given over into Nārada's possession along with precious substances. Nārada then requests a ransom (*nikraya*) in the form of a Kapila cow and her calf, and a black antelope skin packed with sesame and gold. Kr̥ṣṇa buys back his freedom with this payment, blesses Nārada, and Kr̥ṣṇa's other wives come to partake of the blessings of Satyabhāmā's *vrata*. After a year has passed, the *pārijāta* tree is returned to heaven.

The author or authors of this appendix clearly desired to revise the short and uneventful text of *HV* 92.62-70, and to establish the full narrative of war with Indra which as we have seen was already circulating elsewhere in the critical texts of *Mbh* and *HV*, but had not been narrated fully there. Surely so miraculous an object as the *pārijāta* tree could not be had without a vigorous battle, and indeed a recurring rivalry with Indra (in the end, amicable and fraternal rather than truly antagonistic) was already a well-established aspect of Kr̥ṣṇa's character — one thinks immediately of the lifting of Govardhana mountain (*HV* 61) or the burning of Khava forest (*Mbh* 1.214-25). Appendix 29 thus rehabilitates the narrative in accordance with the larger patterns that characterize Kr̥ṣṇa's life and "updates" the short critical text account. Furthermore, the authors of Appendix 29 assigned a very special ritual property to the tree entirely absent in the critical text, thereby endowing the battle for its possession with a distinct religious significance. While at the start of Appendix 29 Satyabhāmā says nothing about rituals, and seems to desire simply to outdo Rukmiṇī, we see in fact that the value of the tree is tied to the *puṇyaka* vow which aims to ensure the long life of a husband and the acquisition of *saubhāgya.*

Indeed, the following Appendix 29A explains very thoroughly how a woman may increase her marital felicity, obtain sons, ensure the long life of her husband, and enhance her physical beauty by all manner of cosmetically-oriented *vrata*s. This emphasis on feminine auspiciousness changes the meaning of the *pārijāta* tree and the battle for its possession. While in the critical *HV* text it is a valuable object, easily obtained in order to beautify Dvārakā, in Appendix 29 it becomes a symbol for and means of acquiring the biological and social wealth which every married woman should cultivate as a mother of sons and wife of a long-lived husband (Austin 2013: 259-65). Kr̥ṣṇa's forcible acquisition of the tree in Appendix 29 is therefore motivated by a desire to assist Satyabhāmā in her ritual and *vrata* activities, and these activities in turn benefit Kr̥ṣṇa as her husband.

Harivaṁśa's Pārijātaharaṇa in Relation to Other Sources

The developments which occur between the critical epic texts and their later appendices, such as Appendix 29, of course do not take place in a vacuum. Rather they represent a very complex and likely centuries-long process of copyists incorporating into their manuscript collections all manner of materials inspired from elsewhere — from other texts of various genres, oral and artistic traditions both performative and plastic, regional and vernacular variations on the stories, and of course from manuscripts of the same text obtained from elsewhere. Two early sources are worth mentioning here in connection with the evolution of *HV*'s Pārijataharaṇa: *Viṣṇu Purāṇa* (*ViP*) and *Harivijaya* of Sarvasena.

ViP likely emerged shortly after the final (i.e. critical-text) forms of *Mbh* and *HV* in the fourth or fifth century CE. It frames Kr̥ṣṇa's biography within a fully articulated theology of Viṣṇu. *ViP*'s Kr̥ṣṇacarita is clearly based upon that of *HV*, but expresses Kr̥ṣṇa's life within a more fully rendered Vaiṣṇava universe. In *ViP*, Satyabhāmā plays a far greater role than in the critical text of *HV*, prompting Kr̥ṣṇa to steal the tree and encouraging her husband to do battle with Indra. They do come to blows over the tree, but then resolve the conflict amicably. Thus in this rendering of the tale, which likely emerged not long after the critical *HV* text, Pārijātaharaṇa is already cast as a battle — a battle prompted by Satyabhāmā — as indeed it always would be thereafter, and as it is in Appendix 29.

A second source is the fifth century CE *Harivijaya* of Sarvasena (Kulkarni 1991: v), likely the first Kāvya work to take up the Pārijātaharaṇa as the theme of an independent poem. This entire work is no longer extant, but has been substantially reconstructed by Kulkarni (1991). In Kulkarni's reconstruction of *Harivijaya* it becomes clear that the poet Sarvasena was not simply rendering the Pārijātaharaṇa as known to him directly into Kāvya verse, but rather was taking some liberties with the episode as it was known to him. It is clear that Sarvasena imported into his rendering of the poem the theme of co-wife jealousy, and that he exploited this for opportunities to describe the envious and charming Satyabhāmā in high Kāvya style. As Kulkarni shows, later poets and theorists such as Ānandavardhana in the ninth century and Abhinavagupta in the tenth and early eleventh centuries praised Sarvasena's exploitation of the Pārijātaharaṇa episode, crediting him with importing the theme of the beautiful, jealous wife which was not part of the original tale. This theme of co-wife jealousy between Rukmiṇī and Satyabhāmā as the driving motivation for the *pārijāta*'s theft then became a stock element in its later expressions. It was he who established the trend of casting the theft of the tree as an adventure driven by the jealous Satyabhāmā.

What these two sources, *ViP* and *Harivijaya*, suggest is that by the time the poets of *HV* Appendix 29 incorporated their extensive retelling of Kṛṣṇa's theft of the tree, there had long been a tradition which understood the event as precipitating a battle, and moreover that this battle had been caused by the jealous Satyabhāmā. The theme of Satyabhāmā as prompter is absent in the critical *HV* (except in so far as Kṛṣṇa looks at her when stealing the tree: *so 'paśyat satyabhāmā . . . HV* 92.66); in *Viṣṇu Purāṇa* (roughly fourth-fifth century) she prompts Kṛṣṇa to steal the tree but is there not driven by co-wife jealousy, only a desire to see Indra proven inferior to her husband. Sarvasena in the fifth century, apparently familiar with *ViP* account, then recast Satyabhāmā and her desire for the tree as a function of jealousy over Rukmiṇī's status, and this then became a popular theme in Kāvya tellings of the Pārijātaharaṇa over the following centuries. By the time the authors of *HV* Appendix 29 added their revision of the Pārijātaharaṇa — perhaps in the tenth or eleventh century — it only made sense to frame the theft of the tree around Satyabhāmā's jealousy. The fact that the authors of Appendix 29 were inspired by Kāvya literature and not other Purānic accounts is clear from the fact that the sulking Satyabhāmā is in Appendix 29 described in the style of the Kāvya genre and not of the much simpler epic *śloka*. However the Appendix 29 poets can themselves be credited with yet another invention and variation of the story, namely the ritual and religious overtones of Satyabhāmā's jealousy and desire for the tree.

Whatever its geographical origins, Appendix 29 became so popular that it made its way into almost every manuscript branch of *HV* across the subcontinent, and into the Vulgate *HV* which constituted the standard edition right up until the early 1970s when Vaidya's critical edition became available.

Kr̥ṣṇa with Rukmiṇī and Satyabhāmā, *kalamkārī*, nineteenth century, Andhra, British Museum

Pārijātaharaṇa in the Sāralā Mahābhārata

Mahendra Kumar Mishra

Mahābhārata is so foundational to the Indian psyche that it has been translated in almost all the *bhāṣās*. In Odisha it is the *Sāralā, Mahābhārata*, a creation of poet Sāralā that occupies an important place in the socio-cultural history of Odisha and remains even today in the collective memory of its people. Even more, it has inspired various arts and rituals in that region. Sāralā was born in the fifteenth century and is celebrated as a central poet of Odisha and he was the first to recast *Mahābhārata* in the language and cultural context of Odisha. In *Sāralā Mahābhārata* Kapilendra Deva, the legendary Gajapati king who ruled during 1435-67, becomes the central figure giving the epic a local flavour.

The poem is written in the *daṇḍī vr̥tta* format which consists of two lines. The letters of one line may not be equal to the other line, but the last letter of the last word of these two lines is phonetically identical. In addition to the mega-narrative of *Mahābhārata* Sāralā includes the episode of Pārijātaharaṇa in his creation.

The Poem

After this, the king of Bilaṅka worshipped at the feet of sage Agastya. Placing flower offerings and with sincere words and folded hands asked:

> O Sage! from where has Devadutta come? What did Indra do with him? How did Viṣṇu slay Narakāsura? Tell me! O Sage, this episode briefly.

Responding to the request of the king, Agastya said:

> O king of Vilaṅka, listen carefully. Hari married sixteen thousand and one hundred women. He killed Narakāsura and liberated these women.

"Please narrate the entire story," the king said. "*Mahābhārata* is nectar for the ears so O king of Vilaṅka! listen attentively."

The demon Narakāsura took the golden umbrella from Varuṇa and snatched the *kalaśa* from the Sun-God Āditya. He attacked the sapphire mountain and Indra was afraid of him. And when messengers gave Indra the news of Kr̥ṣṇa's acts He met the Supreme God Viṣṇu in Dvārikāpura. Hari was in the inner palace of queen Satyabhāmā and Indra met him there. He narrated the atrocities of Narakāsura to Viṣṇu. Kr̥ṣṇa heard Indra attentively and having called Garuḍa in his presence and ordered him:

> Go to Ugrasena and tell him that I have decided to punish Narakāsura. Get ready with eighty-four thousand Yādava soldiers.

Being thus ordered, Garuḍa went and informed Ugrasena. He said:

> Kr̥ṣṇa will punish Narakāsura. Get ready with eighty-four thousand Yādava soldiers without any delay.

Hearing this Ugrasena ordered his soldiers to get ready for war. The soldiers got their weapons ready and the whole universe shivered with war drums, *bherī, mardana, śaṅkha, kāhala, tamaka, niśāna, ḍhola, ḍamalu* and *mardala, ghoṣanāda, dauṇḍi, kada, alabesi, jhāñjala, māhuri, kahalī,* and *baunsī.* This was the battle cry, the noises of horses and the bells of elephants signalled as if a deluge has enveloped the earth. The seven-hooded Vāsuki in Pātāla trembled with this sound and the earth also shook. The herd of soldiers of Yadu, Bhoja, Tuhana, Andhaka, Bamana and Bishnu, all these seven dynasties assembled. There were many great warriors in these seven dynasties. Each of them was incompatible with one another.

After killing the demon the Earth Goddess entreated Kṛṣṇa to give shelter to Bhagadatta. Kṛṣṇa agreed and tied a turban on his head to assure him of protection. After that, Kṛṣṇa went into the palace of Narakāsura, where 16,000 maidens were imprisoned. When Lord Jagannātha saw them, and they also saw His lotus face and each of them thought of getting Him as her own husband. Kṛṣṇa made arrangement for all maidens to be bathed with sandal and offered them nice clothes. He sent those maiden to Dvārakā in palanquins. They all arrived in Dvāravatīpura. There were elephants who owed their pedigree to Airāvata the elephant of heaven. Kṛṣṇa chose sixty-four such elephants and went to Dvārakā. He also took the best horses to Dvārakā. It is said that listening to the story of the killing of the fearful demon Narakāsura all sins will disappear.

Therefore Agastya narrated to the king of Vilaṅka the account of the killing of Narakāsura. After this, the king of Vilaṅka asked sage Agastya, "O great sage! please continue".

Realizing the interest of the king of Vilaṅka to listen to the episode the sage continued with his narration.

O king! directing everybody to Dvārakā, Kṛṣṇa got ready to go to *svarga*. He sat on Garuḍa's back. Kṛṣṇa held a conch, *cakra*, club and a bow, named Taraṅga. His divine body looked like the colour of the lotus. He was adorned with *kaustubha* pearls and gemstones on his neck. The son of Nanda took the figure of Ānanda wearing the ring, bracelet, and *jagadala balaya* armlet decorated with innumerable gemstones. Thus adorned, God appeared on the back of Garuḍa. Satyabhāmā was sitting aside Kṛṣṇa. What a glorious sight it was. They looked like Lakṣmī and Nārāyaṇa. Thirty-three thousand gods were sitting on their *āsanas*. All of them saw Hṛṣikeśa arriving there. Leaving their seats, everybody stood up and all the gods saw Nārāyaṇa. Just as the white cobra is the centre of attraction in the ocean of milk. Kṛṣṇa climbed down from the back of Garuḍa and took his seat.

After that the gods took their seats as well. Satyabhāmā went into the palace led by Śacī. Bṛhaspati asked, "O Kṛṣṇa what is the purpose of your visit to this region?"

God replied:

> We were in Gopapura and after slaying Kaṁsa, we continued towards Mathurā. There we faced the horrific Jarāsandha. He attacked us eighteen times. Attacked by Jarāsandha the Yādavas were stranded in the kingdom and were in trouble.

So I left Mathurā, erecting a hermitage and remained in Dvāravatīpura. You know that we lived with relentless fear of demons.

The gods said:

O Kr̥ṣṇa you are known as the killer of all demons and the saviour of all perils. You have incarnated on earth to diminish the burden of sin. Like a good boatman, please rescue us from the ocean of sorrow of this universe. It is because of you that all the gods exist. You are the friend of devotees, the protector of the world. You came to this heaven, O God-king! and thus it is that we all are secure and safe.

The gods eulogized Kr̥ṣṇa in many ways and with many words.

Kr̥ṣṇa stayed in heaven with Satyabhāmā for some time. Satyabhāmā spent time in heaven with Śacī, the queen of Indra. One day Rambhā, Urvaśī and Menakā, three beautiful court dancers of heaven, met Satyabhāmā. Śacī and others were also present. Just then *pārijāta* flowers were brought there. Musicians playing celestial music gave way to the flower bearers.

When Satyabhāmā saw this she asked Rambhā. "What is the matter? What is this music? Why are people shouting to give way to someone?" Rambhā replied:

O, Goddess, being the queen of God Kr̥ṣṇa do you not know about the *pārijāta*?

Pārijāta is a beautiful flower of heaven, it has a golden glaze. Its fragrance spreads for 500 *yojanas* and it takes one year to blossom. In the second year the leaves of the tree fall. The gardeners take *aṅkoḍi*, a long stick to pluck the flower. This flower is special to Indra as it is used to decorate Śacī's hair everyday. The rest of the flowers when burnt in the fire, mingle in the ocean. Only Indra and Indrāṇī use this flower. This flower emerged during the churning of ocean. This is the best of all trees in heaven, earth and the nether region. It is incomparable. When it is time for flowers to fall they fly to the sky driven by the wind.

Hearing this from Rambhā, Satyabhāmā became happy. She made up her mind to ask Kr̥ṣṇa to take the *pārijāta* tree to Dvāravatīpura. Thinking thus she went to her room. Rambhā, Urvaśī and Menakā also took leave of her.

"O king of Vilaṅka! pay attention to the story that the great sage is recounting." After this the gods went to their respective dwellings. Kr̥ṣṇa also went to the fortress of Indra and after refreshing himself took his *manohi* dinner. Indra along with all the gods reigned in heaven. Kr̥ṣṇa continued to stay in heaven for ten days with Satyabhāmā. Indra and Śacī took utmost care in looking after them. After some days in this place of solitude Satyabhāmā asked Kr̥ṣṇa:

O dear *swāmī*! please pay attention to me. I want to take the *pārijāta* tree to Dvāravatīpura which is my home land.

Kr̥ṣṇa retorted:

O dear queen! this tree is exclusively for Indra. He will not give this tree to others. If you wish, let us go, I will show you the tree.

Kr̥ṣṇa's retinue also followed him in the celestial path. On the banks of the Ākāśagaṅgā there is a garden called Nandana. Just there Satyabhāmā and Kr̥ṣṇa got down from Garuḍa. In the garden neatly planted trees and flowers decorated with eight gemstones were looking beautiful. There the spring wind was blowing even though it was not spring. Soothing winds of this garden would captivate even a sage and even the old become young in this garden. All the beautiful flowers of the fourteen *bhuvanas* grew in this garden. Kr̥ṣṇa with Satyabhāmā entered the garden and finally came near the *pārijāta* tree.

This is an undying tree, wide and full of branches. Each and every leaf takes diverse shapes and its colours change with the seasons. Its *caurā* is 1 *kośa* big. The gemstones in the courtyard dazzle like the mid-noon sun. The four clouds Avartaka, Samvartaka, Drauṇa and Puṣkara always protect the tree and one million sentries guard it. The moon and the sun always protect it. Its flower shines like gold.

Enchanted by the flower Śakravatī (other name of Satyabhāmā) said, "O God! we will take this tree to Dvāravatīpura. I will plant this tree in front of my home". When Kr̥ṣṇa realized that Satyabhāmā is obsessed with the tree He agreed and said, "Alright, we will take this tree". And holding the bottom of the tree Kr̥ṣṇa uprooted it. He kept the tree on the back of Garuḍa and ordered Garuḍa to instantly fly to Dvāravatīpura. The *gandharvas* who were defending the garden reported to Indra about the *pārijāta* tree being taken away by Kr̥ṣṇa. They said, "O king! husband of Śacī, Kr̥ṣṇa has uprooted the *pārijāta* tree and fled to Dvāravatīpura".

Hearing this from the *gandharvas* Indra instantly blocked the way of Kr̥ṣṇa. Indra, seated on Airāvata with his thousand soldiers and their weapons, encircled Kr̥ṣṇa. Indra was angry and ordered the *gandharvas* to follow Him, attack Him from all sides, and kill Him. The soldiers started attacking Kr̥ṣṇa. But Kr̥ṣṇa moved forward fearlessly. Indra, out of anger, called:

> O milkman, halt there, where will you escape? You belong to a lower caste, you are known as Gauḍa, Bauḍa and Hauḍa. You are a criminal for having killed cows. Killer of a woman addicted to liquor — Kādambarī. You tended calves with your cowherds. You did not discriminate your mother's sister, or father's sister, maternal uncle's wife or elder brother's wives. You adored everybody in the forest irrespective of their morality. You are not satisfied with many women. You killed your brother and your nephew. You are a sinner as you killed your father and also the kings. Once you took food from the milkman-Gauḍa. You were there for our first eight years. Innumerable sins have you committed. How should I remind you of your sinful deeds? People call you Nārāyaṇa, that is wrong. The bards have always praised you but today I will see how you will escape. Today the God of death will pull you with his noose. Those who are knowledgeable in thought word and deed are called great.

Jagannātha Kr̥ṣṇa was angry after listening to Indra. He was furious like a fuming cobra, his eyes looked like the *kālacakra*. Biting his lower lips with his teeth He said:

> O Indra! How dare you abuse me? You are a big sinner or an ignorant fool with very little intellect. I am the preserver of this universe. You ill-treated me. Now your time is over and your possession is gone.

Indra said, "that will be ascertained only if you can save your life". Indra was violent. He picked up his Kodaṇḍa bow and with an arrow shot Kr̥ṣṇa. The arrow hit the wings of Garuḍa and it fell down. Indra and all his soldiers surrounded Kṛṣṇa and confronted Him but He all alone successfully conquered them. All the clubs, arrows, spears that the *gandharvas* shot like the raining in Śrāvaṇa hit the body of Garuḍa and turned dust. Garuḍa, son of Vinīta, rumbled like a lion. And all the *gandharvas* ran away from the battlefield in a hurry.

Looking at the cowardly retreat of his soldiers Indra riding his Airāvata confronted his opponents. Jagannātha shot an arrow at the elephant, and it pierced its forehead. With another arrow the mahout was also wounded and pushed back. Garuḍa too attacked the soldiers and they ran away. Garuḍa took the form of Viśvarūpa and his body spread all over the sky and the earth.

With a furious growl like a lion Indra shot arrows after arrows but none of them touched Kṛṣṇa and they became dust. Neither Kṛṣṇa nor Indra were ready to accept defeat or abandon the war. Nārada went to Brahmā and narrated the entire battle.

Hearing this Brahmā went to the battlefield and found it on the banks of Ākāśagaṅgā. Indra and Jagannātha appeared like formidable foes. Seeing this He started eulogizing Kṛṣṇa.

> O God of the Universe! you have taken the *avatāra* of Kṛṣṇa to save the planet. My eyes have been blessed looking at your Viśvarūpa. You have created Indra the god king of heaven but he does not know his limitations, forgive him and stop the battle. You know everything.

Hearing this Kṛṣṇa became happy. Then Brahmā came towards Indra. Seeing Brahmā Indra got down from the elephant. Taking Gaṅgā water in an *aṣṭadhātu kalaśa* he washed Brahmā's feet. He worshipped Brahmā with humility and touched his feet. He said:

> O Grandfather, I am here as the king of heaven because of you. You have given me this wealth and power. I won heaven, earth and the nether region with your blessings. In these three *bhuvanas* there is nobody to defeat me. If my soldiers invade Dvārakāpura they will kill all the Yādavas and uproot Dvārakā. I will plunder his 52 thousand treasures and break the pride of 84 thousand Yādavas.

Hearing this Brahmā was infuriated and said:

> Would you contravene my words and disrupt the path of *dharma*? If a gallant god like you will commit such an unjust act the whole universe will end. Better that you give up, repent, don't follow the devil's path. If you violate my words nothing but evil will befall you.

Hearing this Indra became calm and said:

> Whatever you counsel, O master of Veda, I will follow.

Brahmā said:

> Don't indulge in war with Kṛṣṇa, let them take *pārijāta*. I tell you over and over again, hostility with Kṛṣṇa is not justified. Be patient and listen, all the gods of heaven are his creation by his kindness. I speak with your welfare in mind if you fight with him, you cannot continue. Kṛṣṇa is Nārāyaṇa, he is a great diplomat. He will kill you and also destroy heaven. I will make a truce between you and Govinda or else there is no hope for

> your existence. Kr̥ṣṇa has helped you, this you know. It is better that you leave this place.

Hearing this Indra said, "O master of Veda, how can I overrule your words?" He ordered Aṅgāra Pannaga to call back all the soldiers. For violating Brahmā's word would mean inviting a great disaster.

Hearing this, Aṅgāra Pannaga ordered his troops to stop the battle and return. Indra came back to Amarāvatīkaṭaka. Brahmā went to Kr̥ṣṇa near Ākāśagaṅgā. Looking at Brahmā, Kr̥ṣṇa greeted him and asked how did you do this? Brahmā said, "O Cakrapāṇi, you should enjoy the *pārijāta* flower, but make this earth free from sin, with the help of Arjuna". Go to Dvāravatīpura with the *pārijāta* tree.

Hearing this Kr̥ṣṇa became happy. All the gods offered gifts to Govinda. Everybody worshipped the feet of Jagannātha Nārāyaṇa. He sat on the back of the Garuḍa, bade farewell to the gods and flew away. After going a little while he saw the beautiful city of Dvārakā. It looked like a golden mountain that had fallen from the sky. Garuḍa, with his sound of wings climbed down from the sky to get down in Dvārakā with his master Kr̥ṣṇa and Satyabhāmā with the *pārijāta* tree. Listening to the sound of Garuḍa's descending like a thunderous roar the Yādava clan came and saw that Kr̥ṣṇa had arrived. The nine brothers of Suratha were in Indumatī's palace. They all visited and greeted Kr̥ṣṇa with reverence. Holding the hands of Suratha, God got down from Garuḍa and entered the palace. Paying obeisance to Ugrasena, Kr̥ṣṇa went to Vasudeva and Indumatī worshipped them.

Interpretation

The Pārijātaharaṇa is a pan-Indian narrative found in the main body of *Mahābhārata* and is a part of many regional languages as well. Some common ideas found in this episode can be explored through the text. The main body of the text is all about the glory of Kr̥ṣṇa who is none other than the God Viṣṇu incarnated on Earth to establish *dharma* and abolish demonic acts.

Indra, Br̥haspati and other gods of heaven live a luxurious life, but sometimes their status and power are challenged by demons. The demons attack the gods of heaven and it is the power struggle between gods and demons in their respective spaces. While the gods are dependent on external forces when disturbed by the demons and take shelter, the demons are self-reliant and dominate the earth with their physical force and subjugate the gods. Many gods have little experience to fight the demons, but they take shelter of Brahmā the creator and pursue Viṣṇu the preserver of the Universe to fight evil and safeguard humanity by establishing *dharma*. *Dharma* is a relative term based on two different world-views, one is that of the *deva* and other is that of the *dānava*.

The distribution of power among the demi-gods is dependent on the mercy of the supreme God Viṣṇu. Viṣṇu takes the *avatāra* of Rāma and Kr̥ṣṇa in different times. Kṛṣṇa was the incarnation of Viṣṇu. Knowing that, Indra and the rest of the gods in heaven admired Him and were respectful of Him in heaven when he arrived there with his queen Satyabhāmā. However it was Śacī who was entitled to the *pārijāta*. Satyabhāmā wanted to take the tree. This indicates not only the desire for the flower but also for power.

The episode reveals two basic Purāṇic themes. One is the exercise of power by the demi-gods like Indra against the higher gods like Viṣṇu and the other is the duality of Viṣṇu who is both divine and human at the same time. Viṣṇu as the Supreme God on the one hand protects the gods and saves them from demons. He also assumes different *avatāras* and descends to earth from time to time. After establishing *dharma* Viṣṇu returns to Vaikuṇṭha his heavenly abode. It is interesting that the supremacy and power of Viṣṇu are forgotten and Indra, even though he is well aware of the power of Viṣṇu, forgets his own limitations and takes on Kṛṣṇa in war. On the other hand Kṛṣṇa, Viṣṇu incarnate, also violates the rules of heaven, by forcibly taking the *pārijāta* tree from Indra's garden. He relents to Satyabhāmā's request and steals the *pārijāta*. It shows that even Kṛṣṇa is not free from the influence of his queen. The *pārijāta* in this narrative becomes the symbol of power and status. Satyabhāmā wanted this plant to be in her garden as she wanted to be equal to Śacī and Kṛṣṇa does everything in his power to please her. Brahmā plays his role as the mediator between Kṛṣṇa and Indra when the battle broke out between them for the *pārijāta* tree.

Garuḍa, Vijaynagara, sixteenth century, Shimla Museum of Art

Sāralā Mahābhārata, palm leaf, eighteenth century, Odisha State Museum

Kr̥ṣṇa battles Indra, *paṭacitra*, Odisha, twentieth century

Kr̥ṣṇa battles Indra, Mughal, sixteenth century, Victoria & Albert Museum, London

पारिजात–हरण

नर्मदा प्रसाद उपाध्याय

भारतीय परम्परा में पुष्पों और वृक्षों का देवत्व से अभिन्न संबंध रहा है। यह तथ्य अनेक साक्ष्यों से प्रमाणित है जिनके आधार पर यह ज्ञात होता है कि हमारे ईश्वर, देवों तथा देवियों की पहचान इन पुष्पों तथा वृक्षों से होती रही है।

कृष्ण और इन्द्र का युद्ध, बादामी, ग्यारहवीं सदी

इसका आदर्श उदाहरण वह श्वेत कमल है जिस पर ज्ञान की देवी माँ सरस्वती विराजती हैं। समृद्धि की देवी लक्ष्मी का आसन यदि लाल कमल है तो भगवान् विष्णु की नाभि से निकली कमल–नाल पर खिले कमल–पुष्प पर ब्रह्मा का आसन है।

इसी प्रकार जहाँ तक वृक्षों का प्रश्न है हमारी आँखों के सामने भगवान् कृष्ण का वह अनुराग सामने आता है जो उनका वृक्षों के प्रति था। कृष्ण अपने गोप सखाओं के बीच यदि कदम्ब के वृक्ष के नीचे अपने बचपन में बासुंरी बजाते हैं तो अपने यौवन में महाभारत के युद्ध के समय कुरुक्षेत्र में अर्जुन को विराट् स्वरूप दिखाते हुए कहते हैं कि वृक्षों में अश्वत्थ है और जब उनकी प्रिय पत्नी सत्यभामा पारिजात वृक्ष को ले आने की हठ करती है तो वे इन्द्रलोक से पारिजात के दैवीय वृक्ष को उखाड़कर द्वारिका में स्थापित करते हैं। पारिजात–हरण की यह कृष्णलीला इन्द्र के अहंकार को तोड़ने का संदेश देती है।

पुष्पों और वृक्षों से जुड़ी हुई इस तरह की अनेक कथाएं व मिथक भारतीय साहित्य में मिलते हैं। जिनमें से अनेक तो बहुत लोकप्रिय हैं किन्तु कुछ बहुत कम जिसका उदाहरण पारिजात–हरण का प्रसंग है। यद्यपि पारिजात–हरण का यह प्रसंग भगवान् कृष्ण से जुड़ा हुआ है किन्तु भागवत् के दशम स्कंध की कृष्णलीलाओं की भाँति यह लोकप्रिय नहीं है तथा इसी कारण यह चितेरों और शिल्पियों के आकर्षण का केन्द्र जहाँ एक ओर नहीं रहा वहीं दूसरी ओर भारतीय साहित्य की परम्परा में भी बहुत कम काव्य या नाटक इस प्रसंग को केन्द्र में रखकर रचे गए।

भारतीय धार्मिक प्रसंगों की यह एक महत्त्वपूर्ण विशेषता है कि वे किसी एक अनुशासन में बंधे नहीं रहते। एक प्रसंग यदि चित्रित होता है तो उसे शिल्पकार भी आकार देता है और साहित्यकार भी उसे अपने शब्दों में बांधता है। इन प्रसंगों को कलाकार कभी–कभी अपनी कल्पना से इन्हें परिवर्तित भी कर देता है और विस्तारित भी। पारिजात–हरण का प्रसंग भी इसी संदर्भ में रखा जाना चाहिए। इस कथा का सूत्र तो केवल यह है कि अपनी प्रिय पत्नी सत्यभामा की हठ के कारण इन्द्र को युद्ध में परास्त कर पारिजात का वृक्ष भगवान् कृष्ण इन्द्रलोक से द्वारिका ले आए और उसे सत्यभामा के महल के परिसर में रोप दिया और जब सत्यभामाा का व्रत पूर्ण हो गया तब उस वृक्ष को उन्होंने नारद को दान में दे दिया जिसको उन्होंने पुनः स्वर्गलोक में इन्द्र को लौटा दिया। लेकिन इस कथन को अपने–अपने ढंग से विशेष रूप

से भारतीय साहित्य में वर्णित किया गया है तथा इस पर लघुचित्र भी बने हैं व शिल्प भी।

हमारे पास संस्कृत में इस प्रसंग पर लिखे गए चम्पू काव्य हैं, कुछ ऐसे लघुचित्र हैं जो मुग़ल व पहाड़ी शैलियों पर विशेष रूप से बनाए गए हैं तथा कुछ उदाहरण शिल्पांकन के भी हैं।

पारिजात–हरण का यह प्रसंग *भागवत् पुराण* व *हरिवंश पुराण* के विष्णु पर्व में उल्लिखित है।

ऐसा क्या आकर्षण है इस पारिजात पुष्प में कि जिसके आकर्षण में कृष्ण की प्रिय पत्नी रुक्मिणी व सत्यभामा बंध गईं और सत्यभामा की हठ के कारण कृष्ण को इस वृक्ष को इन्द्रलोक से लाने के लिए इन्द्र से युद्ध करना पड़ा? पारिजात एक ऐसा पुष्प है जिसके अनेक नाम हैं। इसे असमिया में शेवाली, बांग्ला में शेफाली और संस्कृत में निशिपुष्पिका (रात में खिलने वाला पुष्प) कहा जाता है। हिन्दी में इसके प्रचलित नाम हैं, पारिजात, हरसिंगार, शेफालिका, पारिजात्का तथा रागपुष्पिका, आदि।

जैसा कि पूर्व में उल्लेख किया गया है, पारिजात के साथ अन्य कथाएं भी जुड़ी हैं। पारिजात वास्तव में एक दैवीय पुष्प है। यह सौरभ से भरपूर ऐसा पुष्प है जो पूरे परिवेश को पुलक से भर देता है। केवल रात के समय खिलने और उषाकाल में पेड़ के वृन्तों से झरकर धरती पर बिछ जाने वाले सफेद पत्र दलों वाले इस पुष्प की डंडी लाल होती है। इस पुष्प के पत्र–दल बर्फ की तरह सफेद होते हैं। पूरे पुष्प–संसार में केवल यही एकमात्र ऐसा पुष्प है जिसे यह अधिकारिता है कि वह धरती पर झर जाने के बाद भी भगवान् के मस्तक पर चढ़ाया जा सकता है अन्यथा जो पुष्प पेड़ से धरती पर झर जाते हैं उन्हें भगवान् की मूर्ति पर नहीं चढ़ाया जाता।

यह भी कहा जाता है कि यह पुष्प उन देवताओं की देवशैय्या है जो स्वर्ग से धरती पर विचरण करने के लिए आते हैं और इस पारिजात शैय्या पर विश्राम करते हैं। पारिजात का पुष्प जिस पारिजात के वृक्ष पर खिलता है उससे जुड़ी

गरुड़ पर विराजमान विष्णु, पाल, नौवीं सदी

हुई अनेक कथाएं हैं। एक कथा यह भी है कि पारिजातक नामक एक राजकुमारी सूर्य से प्रेम करती थी किन्तु जब उसे अपने प्रेम में असफलता मिली तो उसने आत्महत्या कर ली। उसी की अस्थियों से पारिजात का वृक्ष जन्मा और विकसित हुआ। वह दिन में चूंकि अपने प्रेम का प्रदर्शन नहीं कर सकती इसलिए वह केवल रात को ही फूलती है और सुबह जैसे ही सूर्य उदित होता है आंसू के रूप में उसके पुष्प झरने लगते हैं।

सूर्य की पहली किरणें जैसे ही पारिजात के वृक्ष पर पड़ती हैं उसके फूल आँसुओं के रूप में झरने लगते हैं और धरती पर बिखरकर अपने अमर प्रेम का सौरभ बिखेरते हैं।

यह भी कहा जाता है कि इस वृक्ष का जन्म पाण्डवों की माता कुन्ती की अस्थियों से हुआ तथा अपनी माँ कुन्ती के लिए उनके

वीर पुत्र अर्जुन ने स्वर्ग से यह पारिजात वृक्ष उन्हें लाकर दिया था जिसके फूलों को वे भगवान् शंकर को समर्पित करती थीं।

उत्तर प्रदेश के बाराबंकी ज़िले में किन्तूर नामक एक ग्राम है जिसे महाभारतकालीन कहा जाता है तथा यह मान्यता है कि किन्तूर

गरुड़ पर विराजमान कृष्ण और सत्यभामा, कर्नाटक, बाहरवीं सदी

नाम कुन्ती के नाम पर पड़ा। यहाँ एक प्राचीन व काफी बड़ा पारिजात वृक्ष है जिसके आसपास अनेक मंदिर हैं जिनमें से एक कुन्ती के द्वारा भी बनाया गया बताया जाता है।

जहाँ तक पारिजात–हरण के प्रसंग वर्णन का प्रश्न है, इसका उल्लेख *भागवत पुराण* के पहले व तीसरे अध्याय में है किन्तु विस्तृत विवरण *हरिवंश पुराण* के विष्णु–पर्व में किया गया है। *भागवत पुराण* के प्रथम स्कंध के चौदहवें अध्याय के सैंतीसवें श्लोक में यह प्रसंग उल्लिखित है,

यत्पादशुश्रूषणमुख्यकर्मणा
सत्यादयो द्व्यष्टसहस्त्रयोषितः।
निर्जित्य सङ्ख्ये त्रिदशांस्तदाशिषो
हरन्ति वज्रायुधवल्लभोचिताः।।

जिसका आशय है सत्यभामा आदि सोलह हज़ार रानियां प्रधान रूप से उनके चरण–कमलों की सेवा में रत रहकर उनके द्वारा युद्ध में इंद्रादि देवताओं को भी हराकर इंद्राणी के भोगयोग्य तथा उन्हीं की अभीष्ट पारिजात आदि वस्तुओं का उपभोग करती हैं।

श्रीमद् भागवत के तीसरे स्कंध के तीसरे अध्याय के पाँचवें श्लोक में इस प्रसंग का निम्नानुसार उल्लेख है –

प्रियं प्रभुर्ग्राम्य इव प्रियाया
विधित्सुराच्र्छद्द्युतरुं यदर्थे।
वज्र्याद्रवत्तं सगणो रुषान्धः
क्रीडामृगो नूनमयं वधूनाम्।।

जिसका अर्थ है कि भगवान् विषयी पुरुषों जैसी लीला करते हुए अपनी प्राणप्रिया सत्यभामा को प्रसन्न करने की इच्छापूर्ति के लिए स्वर्ग से कल्पवृक्ष (पारिजात वृक्ष को कल्पवृक्ष भी कहा गया है) को उखाड़ लाए। उस समय इन्द्र ने क्रोध से अंधे होकर अपने सैनिकों सहित उन पर आक्रमण कर दिया क्योंकि वह अपनी स्त्रियों का क्रीड़ामृग बना हुआ था अर्थात् वह उन्हीं के वश में था।

पारिजात के वृक्ष के संबंध में यह मान्यता है कि यह देवों तथा असुरों के द्वारा समुद्र–मंथन के फलस्वरूप प्राप्त हुआ था तथा इस कारण इसे दैवीय वृक्ष कहा जाता है।

प्रचलित कथा के अनुसार एक समय प्रख्यात ऋषि नारद इन्द्रलोक गए तथा उन्होंने वहाँ से कुछ पारिजात पुष्प लाकर भगवान् कृष्ण को द्वारिका में दिए। भगवान् कृष्ण ने उन पुष्पों को अपनी महारानी रुक्मिणी को दिया। नारद ने इस अवसर का लाभ उठाया और वे तुरन्त भगवान् कृष्ण की दूसरी प्रिय पत्नी सत्यभामा

के पास पहुँचे तथा उनसे कहा कि उन्होंने जो पारिजात पुष्प स्वर्ग से लाकर भगवान् कृष्ण को दिए हैं उन पुष्पों को भगवान् कृष्ण ने रुक्मिणी को दे दिया है। यह जानकर सत्यभामा जलन से भर उठीं, तब उन्हें नारद ने यह विकल्प सुझाया कि भगवान् कृष्ण से वे यह आग्रह करें कि वह इन्द्रलोक से पारिजात का वृक्ष लाकर उनके महल में रोप दें। नारद के कहे अनुसार सत्यभामा ने भगवान् कृष्ण से यह हठ की कि वे बजाए कुछ पारिजात के पुष्प लाने के समूचा वृक्ष ही इन्द्रलोक से लाकर उनके महल में रोप दें। सत्यभामा का हठ रोष बन गया। इसी बीच नारद ने इन्द्र को जाकर यह सूचित कर दिया कि इन्द्रलोक से पारिजात वृक्ष को शीघ्र ही चुराया जाएगा। ऐसी स्थिति में भगवान् कृष्ण व उनकी पत्नी सत्यभामा इस वृक्ष को लेने इन्द्रलोक पहुँचे और जब वे इस वृक्ष की कुछ टहनियों को द्वारिका ले जा रहे थे तब इन्द्र से कृष्ण का युद्ध हुआ जिसमें इन्द्र पराजित हुआ और उसने पारिजात वृक्ष को यह शाप दिया कि उसमें कभी फूल नहीं लगेंगे। कृष्ण जब द्वारिका लौटे तब रुक्मिणी को पारिजात पुष्पों को पाने के लिए लालायित कृष्ण ने इस वृक्ष को सत्यभामा के महल में इस तरह रोपा कि जब उसमें फूल आएं तो वे रुक्मिणी के महल के परिसर में गिरें। इस तरह सत्यभामा की यह इच्छा पूर्ण हुई कि उन्हें पारिजात का वृक्ष मिले तथा रुक्मिणी की यह इच्छा पूर्ण हुई कि उन्हें पारिजात के पुष्प।

पारिजात–हरण की यह कथा थोड़े बहुत परिवर्तनों के साथ उल्लिखित है लेकिन जैसा कि पूर्व में कहा गया है कि इसका विस्तृत उल्लेख *हरिवंश पुराण* के विष्णु–पर्व में है। *हरिवंश पुराण* वास्तव में *भागवत पुराण* का ही एक परिशिष्ट है जो हरिवंश–पर्व, विष्णु–पर्व तथा भविष्य–पर्व नाम के तीन पर्वों में विभक्त किया गया है।

जहाँ तक संस्कृत व असमिया साहित्य का प्रश्न है, हमारे सामने इन दोनों भाषाओं पर आधारित कृतियां हैं। सोलहवीं शताब्दी में संस्कृत के कवि शेष श्रीकृष्ण के द्वारा रचा गया "पारिजात–हरण" चम्पू काव्य संस्कृत काव्य की परम्परा में है जो *हरिवंश पुराण* की कथा पर आधारित है।

चम्पू काव्य गद्य व पद्य का मिश्रण है अर्थात् इसमें कविता भी है और बोलचाल के रूप में प्रयुक्त होने वाली वह भाषा भी जिसे गद्य कहा जाता है। संस्कृत में चम्पू काव्य के रचने की परम्परा भी पुरानी है। प्रख्यात परमार राजा भोज ने दसवीं सदी में *चम्पू रामायण* की रचना की थी। संस्कृत में दसवीं सदी के पूर्व में चम्पू काव्य प्राप्त नहीं होते थे। विद्वानों का यह कहना है कि संस्कृत में चम्पू काव्य की यह परम्परा बौद्ध जातकों से आई है। संस्कृत में सर्वाधिक पुराना चम्पू *नल चम्पू* है जिसे भट्ट त्रिविक्रम के द्वारा रचा गया। इसके बाद जैन परम्परा में सोमदेव सूरी ने दसवीं सदी में *यशस्तिलक* नामक चम्पू काव्य की रचना की।

दसवीं सदी के बाद भी यह परम्परा निरन्तर विद्यमान रही तथा इसी परम्परा में "पारिजात–हरण" काव्य की रचना हुई। यह काव्य ललित भाषा में लिखा गया तथा प्रकाशित है। यह भी कहा जाता है कि यह कृति राजा नरोत्तम के समय रची गई थी जो काशी के निकट तंडकपुर के नरेश के भाई थे। पारिजात–हरण के प्रसंग पर केन्द्रित यह चम्पू काव्य पाँच अध्यायों में विभक्त है तथा पाँचवें अध्याय में इसका समापन होता है। इस चम्पू काव्य में वर्णित कथानक के अनुसार भगवान् कृष्ण व इन्द्र दोनों भाई थे तथा उनके बीच पारिजात को लेकर हुए युद्ध को समाप्त कराने के लिए युद्ध–क्षेत्र में इन्द्र के गुरु बृहस्पति पहुँचे। यह युद्ध पारियात्र पर्वत पर हो रहा था। गुरु बृहस्पति की सलाह मानी गई तथा भगवान् कृष्ण जब इस वृक्ष

को लेकर द्वारिका पहुँचे तब सत्यभामा ने अपने द्वारा रखे गए व्रत को तोड़ा। जब व्रत से संबंधित समस्त रीतियां पूर्ण हो गईं तब सत्यभामा ने इस वृक्ष का दान नारद को कर दिया जिसे उन्होंने पुनः इन्द्रलोक पहुँचा दिया।

उक्त के अतिरिक्त "पारिजात–मंजरी", "पारिजात–नाटक" तथा "पारिजात–लता" नामक काव्य भी इस प्रसंग को केन्द्र में रखकर रचे गए। संस्कृत के रचनाकार गोपालदास तथा दिवाकर ने "पारिजात–हरण" नामक काव्यों की रचना की। इसके अलावा कबीर, नरेन, रघुनाथ तथा उमापति ने भी इस प्रसंग पर काव्य तथा नाटक रचे। इनमें से उमापति द्वारा रचा गया "पारिजात–नाटक" प्रसिद्ध है। यह संस्कृत–मिश्रित मैथिली में रचा गया है। ये सभी उत्तर मध्यकालीन रचनाएं हैं। पिछली सदी में पण्डित उमापति द्विवेदी नामक कवि ने भी एक "पारिजात–हरण" नामक काव्य की रचना की है। वर्ष 1962 में पण्डित त्रिनाथ शर्मा ने "पारिजात–हरण चम्पू" की व्याख्या की जिसका प्रकाशन चौखम्बा विद्या भवन बनारस से हुआ है।

जैसा कि पूर्व में उल्लेख किया गया है आसाम में मध्यकाल के प्रख्यात कवि शंकरदेव के द्वारा "पारिजात–हरण" नामक ग्रंथ रचा गया। वे एक वैष्णव भक्त थे तथा अपने समय के प्रख्यात कवि भी थे। उन्होंने आसाम में भक्ति आन्दोलन चलाया तथा *रामायण* सहित *भागवत* के कुछ अंशों का अनुवाद किया।

उन्होंने कुल 27 ग्रंथों की रचना की। उन्हें यह भी श्रेय दिया जाता है कि उन्होंने आसाम में "अंकिया–नट" नामक नाटक के एक प्रकार तथा "वारगिट" नामक कविता के एक रूप की रचना की। उन्होंने "रुक्मिणी–हरण" नामक काव्य भी रचा। पारिजात–हरण के प्रसंग पर अनेक भाषाओं में भी रचनाएं हैं लेकिन उनके

कृष्ण और इन्द्र का युद्ध, टैराकोटा, बिष्णुपुर, उन्नीसवीं सदी

संबंध में विस्तृत विवेचन उपलब्ध नहीं है। यह अवश्य है कि इस प्रसंग पर आधारित नाटकों का मंचन वर्तमान समय में प्रायः किया जाता है।

जहाँ तक चित्रांकन परम्परा का प्रश्न है, मुग़ल कलम में अकबर के समय में सत्रहवीं सदी में *हरिवंश पुराण* का सचित्र अंकन किया गया था। *हरिवंश पुराण* का अनुवाद भी अकबर के समय में किया गया था। इस प्रसंग पर आधारित मुग़ल कलम का एक सुंदर अंकन विक्टोरिया एण्ड अलबर्ट म्यूज़ियम ऑफ लंदन में है।

सामान्यतः गढ़वाल कलम में इस प्रसंग को चित्रित किया गया है। इस प्रसंग पर आधारित दो लघुचित्र उपलब्ध हैं। एक चित्र में इस प्रसंग से संबंधित विभिन्न दृश्यों को चित्रित किया गया है। गढ़वाल कलम के अन्य पारम्परिक चित्रों में हुए अंकनों के अनुसार इस चित्र को भी विभिन्न भागों में विभक्त किया गया है। इस अंकन की महत्त्वपूर्ण विशेषता यह है कि इसमें झरोखों को निर्मित किया गया है जिनमें विभिन्न भंगिमाओं में कृष्ण अंकित हैं। यह बहुत संभव है कि यह अंकन गढ़वाल के प्रख्यात चितेरे भोलाराम का हो। यह अंकन अठारहवीं सदी के उत्तरार्द्ध का प्रतीत होता है। इसका साम्य रुक्मिणी–हरण के उस अंकन से होता है जो गेयर एण्डरसन संग्रह नैशनल गैलरी ऑफ ऑस्ट्रेलिया कैनबरा में संरक्षित है।

इसी प्रकार व इसी अवधि का एक और अंकन पहाड़ी कलम का मौजूद है। इस अंकन में

गरुड़ पर विराजमान विष्णु, पाल, दसवीं सदी

पारिजात वृक्ष को सत्यभामा के महल के परिसर में रोपते हुए चित्रित किया गया है। यह कांगड़ा शैली का अठारहवीं सदी का अंकन है जो राष्ट्रीय संग्रहालय, नई दिल्ली में संग्रहीत है।

राष्ट्रीय संग्रहालय नई दिल्ली में संरक्षित कांगड़ा शैली के एक लघुचित्र में पारिजात वृक्ष के द्वारिका में लाए जाने के अवसर पर द्वारिका की महिलाओं द्वारा उसके देखे जाने की घटना को चित्रित किया गया है। यह अंकन अठारहवीं सदी का है।

कांगड़ा शैली में ही अठारहवीं सदी का एक और अंकन है जो राष्ट्रीय संग्रहालय नई दिल्ली में संरक्षित है। इसमें भगवान् कृष्ण, सत्यभामा को सांत्वना देते हुए दर्शाए गए हैं।

पहाड़ी शैली में किया गया सुंदर अंकन जो संभवतः चम्बा कलम का अठारहवीं सदी का है वह चंडीगढ़ के राजकीय संग्रहालय में संग्रहीत है। अठारहवीं सदी में किए गए इस अंकन में पारिजात के वृक्ष को उखाड़कर कृष्ण के द्वारा इसे ले जाते हुए चित्रित किया गया है। गरुड़ को भी इस अंकन में चित्रित किया गया है जो कृष्ण के पीछे हाथ जोड़े जा रहे हैं। इस अंकन में इन्द्र को भी दर्शाया गया है जो कृष्ण को रोकने का प्रयास कर रहे हैं।

पहाड़ी कलम में सत्यभामा के द्वारा पुण्यक व्रत को मनाने के भी अंकन किए गए हैं। यह अंकन भी अठारहवीं सदी के हैं। इनमें से दो व्यक्तिगत संग्रहों में हैं।

आगरा–देहली कलम में सोलहवीं सदी में किए गए एक सुन्दर अंकन को लॉस एन्जिलिस काउण्टी म्यूज़ियम ऑफ आर्ट अमेरिका में संरक्षित किया गया है। इस अंकन में वायुमार्ग से गरुड़ अपने मस्तक पर सिंहासन में विराजे कृष्ण और सत्यभामा को ले जाते हुए दर्शाए गए हैं। चित्र के एक दूसरे भाग में कृष्ण को पारिजात वृक्ष को उखाड़ते हुए चित्रित किया गया है। यह अंकन मीठाराम भागवत के अंकन के समान है।

इस प्रसंग पर आधारित कुछ और लघुचित्रों के होने की सूचनाएं हैं किन्तु जैसा कि पूर्व में उल्लिखित किया गया है, यह प्रसंग चितेरों तथा शिल्पियों का लोकप्रिय विषय नहीं रहा। इस कारण इस प्रसंग पर आधारित रूपायन व शिल्पांकन काफी कम है।

आसाम में पारिजात–हरण के प्रसंग पर शंकरदेव ने यदि काव्य रचना की तो बाद के समय में सचित्र ग्रंथों के सृजन की परम्परा निरन्तर चली जिसमें राजस्थानी व मुग़ल शैली का समन्वित रूप भी दिखाई दिया। शंकरदेव ने पारिजात–हरण का जो विवेचन किया वह परवर्ती काल में आसाम के चितेरों की प्रेरणा बना। ईस्वी सन् 1896 में वहाँ सचित्र *ब्रह्मवैवर्त्त*

पुराण रचा गया व उसी शैली में जिसे ससधारा के नाम से भी जाना जाता है पारिजात–हरण के प्रसंग को चित्रित किया गया है।

जहाँ तक शिल्पांकन का प्रश्न है, कृष्णलीला के आधार पर शिल्पांकन अपेक्षाकृत कम हैं। कृष्णलीला के शिल्पांकन का सबसे पुराना उदाहरण ईस्वी पूर्व पहली या दूसरी सदी का मथुरा में मिला है। मथुरा के गायत्री टीले से मिले इस अंकन में वासुदेव के द्वारा सद्यजात कृष्ण को अपने सिर पर रखे हुए यमुना पार ले जाते हुए दिखाया गया है। बाद की अवधि में कृष्णलीला के शिल्पांकनों के उदाहरण पहाड़पुर सहित बीकानेर, मांडोर, बनारस तथा बादामी में मिले हैं।

कृष्णलीला के अंकनों में अनेक पैनल विदिशा में भी मिले हैं। मुरैना से लाए ऐसे सुंदर पैनल वर्तमान में ग्वालियर संग्रहालय में भी हैं तथा झालावाड़ के सुप्रसिद्ध सूर्य मंदिर की दीवारों पर भी ऐसे अंकन मौजूद हैं। ये सभी अंकन दसवीं सदी के पूर्व के हैं किन्तु इन पर अभी तक किसी सजग शोधार्थी की दृष्टि नहीं पड़ी है। इन सभी में बादामी की गुफाओं के अंकन प्रसिद्ध हुए हैं।

बादामी की गुफाएं उत्तरी कर्नाटक में बागलकोट ज़िले में हैं। इन गुफाओं को पहाड़ की चट्टानों को काटकर बनाया गया है। ईसा पूर्व के बाद की छठवीं से आठवीं सदी के बीच इस क्षेत्र पर शासन करने वाले चालुक्य राजाओं की राजधानी बादामी थी। यहाँ मिले एक शिलालेख के अनुसार इसका निर्माण शक् संवत 500–78 ई. बीच हुआ। बादामी की गुफा क्रमांक 4 के आधार–स्थान पर कृष्णलीला के अंकन हैं। इस आधार–स्थान में कृष्ण तथा इन्द्र के मध्य युद्ध को दर्शाया गया है। इस दृश्य में देवता दाहिनी ओर खड़े हुए हैं। अन्य उत्कीर्णनों से यह उत्कीर्णन पृथक्

गरुड़ पर विराजमान विष्णु, कर्नाटक, अठारहवीं सदी

किया गया है। इस दृश्यांकन में गरुड़ की पीठ पर बैठे हुए कृष्ण दाहिनी दिशा में बाणों की वर्षा कर रहे हैं। कृष्ण के सामने भी एक व्यक्ति को उनसे युद्धरत् दर्शाया गया है तथा उसी के निकट एक अन्य व्यक्ति को तलवार की तरह के हथियार के साथ शिल्पित किया गया है। पैनल के मध्य में इसी आधार–स्थान में एक अंकन है जिसमें पारिजात वृक्ष को भी शिल्पित किया गया है। एक महिला को भी इस वृक्ष को प्रणाम करते हुए दर्शाया गया है। इस दृश्य में कृष्ण भी दिखाई देते हैं। बादामी की गुफाओं के ये अंकन विशेष रूप से इसलिए भी महत्त्वपूर्ण हैं क्योंकि ये दक्षिण भारत में अवस्थित गुफाओं में बने हुए हैं। जबकि इस काल में कृष्णलीला का प्रचार व प्रसार उत्तर भारत की अपेक्षा कम रहा होगा।

इस प्रसंग के अंकन का एक महत्त्वपूर्ण उदाहरण जो उन्नीसवीं सदी का है वह पश्चिम बंगाल में टैराकोटा में मिलता है। बंगाल में ईंटों से बनाए

मंदिर बहुतायत में मिलते हैं तथा मंदिरों में मिट्टी के शिल्प का ऐसा अद्वितीय व अद्भुत सौन्दर्य दिखाई देता है जो संभवतः भारत में अन्यत्र नहीं है।

अधोसंरचना तथा उसके अलंकरण के संबंध में प्रयोग बंगाल में सत्रहवीं तथा अठारहवीं सदी में बहुत हुए तथा एक समय ऐसा आया जब इनके प्रमाण सुनिश्चित हो गए लेकिन चित्रांकन की शैलियों में जिस तरह आंचलिक तत्त्वों के विद्यमान रहने से उनकी विविधता भी रहती है वैसा ही वैविध्य बंगाल के उन्नीसवीं सदी में बने इन मंदिरों की संरचनाओं में हुआ।

अठारहवीं सदी तक समृद्ध अलंकरण वाली एक सुनिश्चित शैली पश्चिम बंगाल में विशेष रूप से हुगली तथा हावड़ा के अंचलों में स्थिर हो चुकी थी तथा इन मंदिरों के शिल्प पर शोध करने वाले संस्कृतिविद् श्री अमित गुहा ने यह सूचित किया है कि अन्य विषयों जैसे दरबार व शिकार दृश्यों के अंकनों के साथ–साथ *रामायण* व कृष्णलीला के प्रसंगों पर आधारित अंकन हुए।

हुबली ज़िले में आराम बाग के निकट बारूल के रघुनाथ मंदिर में इस काल में हुई कृष्णलीला के सर्वश्रेष्ठ अंकन हैं। इसी प्रकार के अन्य मंदिरों में से एक मंदिर विशनपुर का है जिसमें भित्तियों पर निर्मित कृष्णलीला के शिल्पों में प्रयोगात्मकता दिखाई देती है। मुर्शिदाबाद के निकट के रानी भवानी मंदिर व मेदिनीपुर मंदिर के पुथिया तथा कांतानगर के मंदिरों की दीवारों पर शिल्पांकित कृष्णलीला भी विशेष रूप से दर्शनीय है।

उन्नीसवीं सदी में परम्परागत रूप से कृष्णलीला के जो शिल्पांकन इन मंदिरों में हुए उनकी शैली में बदलाव आया जिसके उदाहरण देवीपुर मंदिर की भित्तियों पर शिल्पांकित पारिजात–हरण का प्रसंग है इसमें इन्द्र तथा कृष्ण के युद्ध को जीवन्त रूप में उरेहा गया है। टैराकोटा में किया गया यह शिल्पांकन अपने आप में संभवतः विश्व में इस प्रसंग का प्रतिनिधि उदारण कहा जा सकता है। युद्ध करते इन्द्र व कृष्ण की भंगिमाएं आनुपातिक रूप से उरेही गई हैं। दोनों की देह–यष्टियों का आकार यद्यपि ठिगना है किन्तु वे संतुलित हैं। उनकी गतिशीलता देखते ही बनती है। पारिजात के वृक्ष का अंकन भी गैर–पारम्परिक है। वृक्ष को छोटा किन्तु सुन्दर बनाया गया है। बंगाल की शिल्प प्रतिभा मानो इस अंकन में मुखर हो उठी है।

उक्त विवेचन से यह स्पष्ट होता है कि *भागवत पुराण* तथा *हरिवंश पुराण* के विष्णु–पर्व में उल्लेखित पारिजात–हरण का यह प्रसंग भले साहित्य, शिल्प व चित्रांकन परम्परा में साहित्यकारों व कलाकारों के बीच कम लोकप्रिय रहा हो किन्तु वह उपेक्षित नहीं रहा। इस छोटे से प्रसंग का यही संदेश है कि अहंकार चाहे इन्द्रलोक के अधिपति का ही क्यों न हो वह अंततः समाप्त होता ही है। अभिमान की कभी विजय नहीं होती तथा सच्चे प्रयत्न में इतनी सामर्थ्य होती है कि वह स्वर्ग की संपदा को भी अपने पौरुष के बल पर देवलोक से इस भूलोक पर ला सकता है।

पारिजात का वृक्ष मनुष्य के पुरुषार्थ की निधि है न कि देवों की संपदा।

Chamba *rūmāl*, twentieth century, Dehejia Collection of Kṛṣṇa Art

A Visual Narrative

Harsha V. Dehejia

The narrative of Pārijātaharaṇa begins with the marriage of Kṛṣṇa and Satyabhāmā. Sūrya gifted *syamantaka*, a dazzling jewel to Satrajit. His brother Prasena borrowed this jewel but was killed by a lion in the cave of Jāmbavān. Satrajit suspects Kṛṣṇa for the foul play and Kṛṣṇa battles the bear demon Jambavan. After a prolonged fight Jāmbavān concedes defeat and offers to give the jewel and his daughter Satyabhāmā in marriage to Kṛṣṇa. Kṛṣṇa graciously accepts the hand

1

2

of Satyabhāmā but asks Jāmbavān to keep *syamantaka*. The wedding of Kṛṣṇa and Satyabhāmā was a modest event. Satyabhāmā was dressed in a simple attire. The marriage pavilion was made up of simple poles and a festoon of leaves. The officiating priest was a brāhmaṇa by the name of Kulaka.

In times of yore the great sage Kaśyapa was pleased with the devotion of Aditi and asked her for a boon. Aditi asked for a boon that would always keep her virtuous and prosperous, that she be adorned at all times, be surrounded by music and dance, look young, free of sorrow and devoted to her husband and *dharma*. Kaśyapa bestowed a boon on Aditi and created

3

4

the *pārijāta*. The *pārijāta* tree had three branches and bore fruits of all the celestial trees and such were its qualities that it would attract everyone. Kaśyapa created this tree with the essence of the *mandara* tree and therefore it was considered the best of all the trees. The *pārijāta* arose on the banks of the Viṣṇupadī and was also called *mandara*. Since people asked what kind of a tree it is, it is also called *kovidara*.

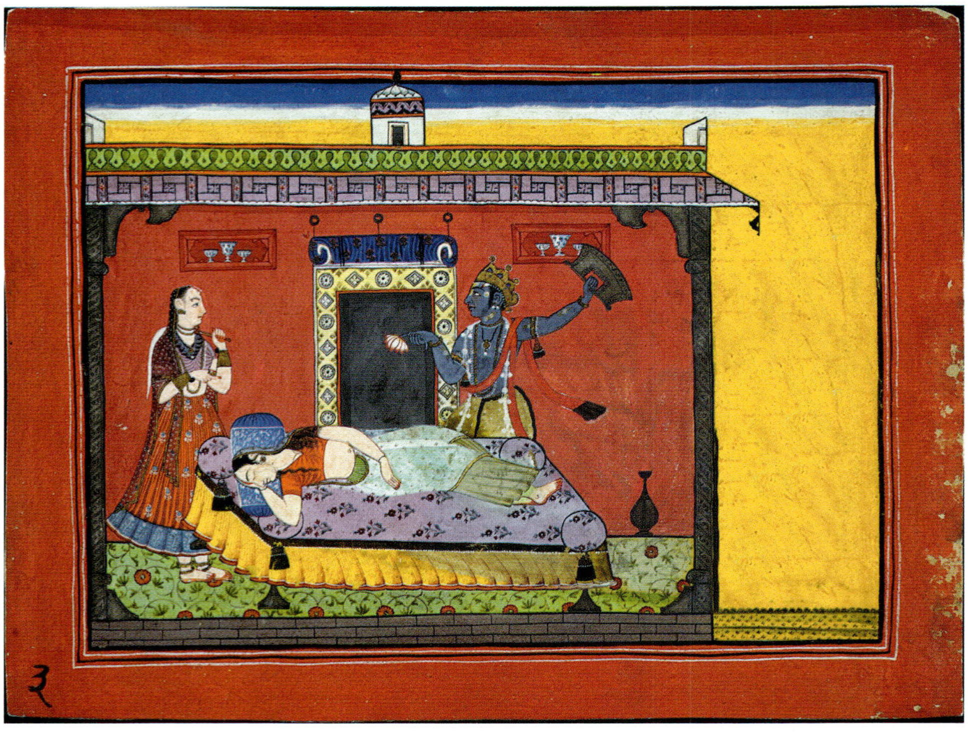

5

6

After his marriage Kṛṣṇa went to the Revantaka mountain with Rukmiṇī. When Kṛṣṇa was seated there along with Rukmiṇī and other spouses Nārada approached him and offered him a *pārijāta* flower and Kṛṣṇa handed this to Rukmiṇī and she put it in her hair and she looked very beautiful.

7

8

Nārada told Rukmiṇī: "This flower remains fresh for a year and does not fade. It keeps you warm and cool depending on the season and fulfils all your desires. Its fragrance pleases the mind and enhances virtues. It gives you whatever you desire. It bestows good fortune and its fragrance protects the mind from the evil path. It changes its colour, size and weight as you wish. It removes bad odours and sheds light at night. With its flowers one can create garlands, pavilions and costumes of flowers. It removes hunger, old age and sadness. It brings sweet music to your ears. At the end of a

9

10

year, the flowers disappear and goes back to the tree. Umā, the beloved of Śiva always uses these flowers. The *pārijāta* is better than the gems of all the three worlds." Nārada then reported the event to Satyabhāmā.

Later when Kr̥ṣṇa went to the home of Satyabhāmā which was built on the Revantaka mountain by Viśvakarmā. Satyabhāmā was petulant, holding a lotus to her mouth and drawing lines on the ground with her feet. The fragrance of the *pārijāta* wafted when Kr̥ṣṇa entered the room. Satyabhāmā asked her maids where the fragrance was coming from. With eyes choked with tears she told Kr̥ṣṇa that it was not proper for such a fragrance to come from his body. Kr̥ṣṇa looking graceful with his lotus-like eyes embraced Satyabhāmā and

11

12

13

asked why there were tears, which resembled dew drops from lotus leaves. Your face resembles the grace of the rising sun then why is it looking like the faded lotus in the evening? Why are you dressed in white clothes and devoid of ornaments? What wrong have I done to you that you are so troubled? You are as beautiful as an *apsaras* and my love for you will last even after my death. Satyabhāmā said until today I felt that you belong to me but now I do not feel that way. I have become a laughing stock of the world as well as among my co-wives as you gave the *pārijāta* flower to your beloved Rukmiṇī. I have fallen from grace, how could then I witness the glory of the Revatanka blossoming with flowers? Kr̥ṣṇa, I never thought that you would be so wicked and deceitful. Your true nature has been exposed today.

Kr̥ṣṇa said that Nārada gave him the *pārijāta* flower and He in turn gave it to Rukmiṇī. If you want it then I shall bring the *pārijāta* tree from heaven and plant it in your home.

Saying that, Kr̥ṣṇa summoned Nārada and Satyabhāmā honoured him by washing his feet. Nārada requested permission to return to Indraloka where a programme of music and dance is held every month in honour of Śiva. Having taken leave of Aditi, Kr̥ṣṇa and Satyabhāmā mounted

14

Garuḍa. From the air they saw Nandana, the garden of Indra which had a sweet fragrance. Seeing this Satyabhāmā asked Kṛṣṇa to take her there as she wanted to enjoy it. Kṛṣṇa alighted from Garuḍa and entered the garden which was guarded by Indra's men. She saw in that garden beautiful trees bent down with fruits, resonating with intoxicated bees and covered with the dust of flowers.

Just then Satyabhāmā saw the *pārijāta* tree and struck by its beauty asked Kṛṣṇa what it was. Kṛṣṇa said that this is a tree of heaven. The space around the bottom is paved with coral, its trunk is golden, its leaves are of sapphire, the railing around it is of lapis lazuli, its flowers are of ruby and its fruits are of *gomeda*, it shines with flower filaments of diamonds and its branches are of emeralds. Satyabhāmā said that she loved this tree and that it should be taken to Dvārakā at

15

16

which Kṛṣṇa explained that it could not be removed as the tree was given to Indra when it arose from the churning of the ocean. Satyabhāmā was petulant and said that if Kṛṣṇa loved her he should get the tree.

Kṛṣṇa acceded to her wishes and asked Nārada to go and inform Indra of his decision to take the *pārijāta* tree. When Indra heard Kṛṣṇa's message he said that he would not part with the *pārijāta* and would wage a war with Kṛṣṇa. Nārada conveyed this to Kṛṣṇa.

On hearing that Kṛṣṇa said that Indra would not be able to stand a war with him and that he has firmly resolved to carry the *pārijāta* tree. Indra went to Bṛhaspati who advised him to get ready for war along with Jayanta. Bṛhaspati went to the shore of

17

18

the milky ocean and spoke to Kaśyapa. Kaśyapa said that the war is inevitable and you should be present there. Śiva asked Kaśyapa to go to heaven along with Aditi to protect both Indra and Kr̥ṣṇa.

Confronted by Indra, Kr̥ṣṇa said, "Your daughter-in-law desires this tree and I am taking it for her", hearing which Indra said that he could not take it without a fight. Indra summoned all the gods and prepared for the battle. Indra mounted the Airāvata, Agni rode a horse, Yama got on to his buffalo, Nirr̥ti was carried by a man, Varuṇa sat on an alligator, Vāyu chose a black antelope, Kubera was in a palanquin, Śiva was on his bull. There were sounds of drums, cymbals, *mr̥daṅgas* and kettledrums and loud shouting and roaring was also heard.

19

20

Kṛṣṇa shot arrows at Airāvata and Indra in turn wounded Garuḍa with arrows. Jayanta tried to take away the *pārijāta* forcibly but Pradyumna stopped him and a violent fight took place between the two of them. Pravara, friend of Indra and invisible because of the boon of Brahmā, tried to rescue the *pārijāta*. Pravara wounded Sātyaki and Sātyaki in turn cut off his bow.

21

22

Using his wings Garuḍa threw off Pravara. Pradyumna stood to the left of the *pārijāta* and Sātyaki to the right. Garuḍa, son of Kaśyapa, attacked Airāvata and he fell. Kr̥ṣṇa went to the Pariyātra mountain along with Garuḍa. Pradyumna and Sātyaki were sitting on Garuḍa. Indra was in the chariot with Jayanta and shot arrows and Kr̥ṣṇa in turn attacked Airāvata. The earth shook, stars from the sky fell, serpents of the nether world got agitated.

Brahmā asked Kaśyapa to intervene in the battle between Indra and Kr̥ṣṇa and Aditi asked them to stop fighting. She suggested that if Kr̥ṣṇa wanted the *pārijāta,* He could take it to Dvārakā and perform the *puṇyaka vrata* and after that

23

24

25

26

repatriate the tree to Nandana. Kṛṣṇa then uprooted the tree and prepared to go to Dvārakā.

Śacī gave many coloured gems to Kṛṣṇa for his many wives. Kṛṣṇa asked Sātyaki to inform the people of Dvārakā that he had brought the *pārijāta* tree. Pradyumna entered Dvārakā with the tree. Seeing the tree everyone in Dvārakā were delighted. The blind regained their sight, the ailing were cured, the old became young, birds enjoyed love sports. Satyabhāmā

27

28

was delighted and started preparing for the *puṇyaka vrata*.

Satyabhāmā placed a garland of flowers and tied Kr̥ṣṇa to the *pārijāta* tree.

Then she donated Kr̥ṣṇa to Nārada with the oblation of water, a thousand cows and a mountain of gold. Kr̥ṣṇa blessed Nārada. It was Umā who had first revealed the method of carrying out the *puṇyaka vrata*. At that *vrata* all the daughters of Prajāpati, all the rivers, daughters of the mountains, wife of Agni, all the goddesses were present and Umā honoured them. Arundhatī, the daughter of Soma, asked Umā to narrate to the assembled people the method of carrying out this *vrata*.

Umā accepted the request and said that it was Śiva who taught her the *vrata*. *Puṇyaka vrata* is for women who want to remain chaste and attached to *dharma*. During the *vrata* the wife should remain devoted to her husband, wear white clothes and should not use perfumes.

Eleven chaste women should be invited to the *vrata*. She should observe a fast on that day and bathe in the river or in step wells filled with lotus flowers. Taking a copper vessel filled with unbroken rice and *kuśa* grass she should wash the right horn of a cow and drink that water.

29

She should then recite *mantras* and ask the sun and the moon to be her witness. And then she should tie her husband and sell him.

After this the woman should present gifts to the brāhmaṇa. These should include food, clothes, gems. Salt, butter, sugar-cane balls, honey and the images of Umā–Maheśvara made of gold should also be given. A vase full of sesame seeds and a white cow should be given away as charity. O Arundhatī! I was the first to perform this *vrata* and because of this it has come to be known as Umāvrata on earth. This is the best of all the *vratas* and when it is combined with charitable acts, a woman gets all her desires fulfilled. O beautiful one! because of the *vrata* it appears as if I have purchased Lord Śiva.

Thus, the *vrata* was explained to the assembled gathering. Everyone present was pleased. Nārada in particular was touched by the devotion of everyone who attended.

30

Harsha V. Dehejia

Chamba Kalam 3, 4, 5, 9, 10, 18, 24, 27, 28 (Government Museum and Art Gallery, Chandigarh)

These paintings according to Vijay Sharma belong to the Chamba atelier. The idioms and traits of this mature and well-established painting style that had developed during Rājā Chhatra Singh's period continued in the reign of his son and successor Rājā Udai Singh (1690–1720). An inscribed and dated breastplate, locally called *kañcua* (Sanskrit *kavaca*), is seen as an armour on the torso of the idol of Lakṣmī-Nārāyaṇa, the principal deity of Chamba. This breastplate is important for two reasons: first, the inscription is dated (CE 1715) and bears the name of Rājā Udai Singh, the donor, on whose instance the plate was re-made and offered to the deity, and second, for the remarkable draftsmanship of the figural work embossed upon it. The figures engraved on the breastplate bear a remarkable stylistic similarity to the ones in the paintings. The paintings of Pārijātaharaṇa from the Chandigarh Museum, presented in this portfolio bear stylistic resemblance to the figures in the breastplate. One notices the male figures seen in the Pārijātaharaṇa series wearing a typical crown with triangular motif and *dhotī* with a particular kind of shading using parallel lines. These figures have long horizontal *tilaka* marks on their broad foreheads, which is a characteristic of the Chamba paintings of this period. In the female figures clad in collared *colī* and flared *ghāgharā*, a three-stringed-beaded necklace, *campākalī*, which is worn tight around the neck, along with a two-stringed necklace of gold and pearls. The round chubby faces, the elongated almond-shaped eyes with reddish corners, and circular forms indicating the prominent chest muscles of the male figures are invariably noticed in miniatures of the late seventeenth-century Chamba paintings. These traits continued in practice in the Chamba painting style, though in a slightly refined manner, until the mid-eighteenth century.

Pālam Bhāgavata 19 (San Diego Museum), 20 (Museum of Fine Arts, Boston), 22 (Los Angeles County Museum of Art)

Bhāgavata Purāṇa series from the first half of the sixteenth century (1525-40) is an important document in the history of Indian painting. Not only is it the earliest known illustrated manuscript of *Bhāgavata* but it is probably the largest with about 300 folios. It seems clear that this must have emerged from an active and vibrant atelier, probably patronized by a Hindu merchant and not a king. There is some evidence that the merchant belonged to the Puṣṭi-Mārga Sampradāya and some have even suggested that Viṭṭhalanātha himself had a role to play in its creation. Two names that appear in this manuscript are those of Mīṭhārāma and Nānā who may have been brothers who owned this at one time. In one inscription the name Pālam appears suggesting that the atelier was in a suburb of Delhi. The paintings have a flat red background with figures that have pronounced eyes, a skyline with a wavy cloud line. The predominant colours are red and yellow. The architecture with festoons and textile awnings resembles Sultanate structures. The triangular *paṭakās* and the patterned clothes worn by the women are reminiscent of the Caurapañcāśikā style of paintings and it is this which have led some scholars to suggest that this pre-Mughal style of painting originated in Gwalior where carved dancing figures in the Caura style of dress are seen carved in the Gwalior Fort. The men wear *dhotī*s along with a *paṭakā* and the characteristic *kuladhar* headdress. There is about this *Bhāgavata* manuscript a certain animation, a bold representation, a vibrant and dynamic ethos which make it a unique manuscript. This series is important not only for its antiquity but for it seems to have originated not from a royal atelier but from the patronage of a Hindu merchant suggesting that there was patronage for painting even before the Mughal and later Rājpūt ateliers.

Early Kāṅgṛā
6, 7 (Ramesh Kapoor Collection)

The Kapoor painting is from the eighteenth century Kāṅgṛā *kalam* and is perhaps from a third generation of the Seu family probably under the patronage of Rājā Ghamaṇḍa Chand (r. 1751-74). The early Kāṅgṛā *kalam* has some resemblances to the Basohli style particularly in its bold and staring eyes and coarse female features. It is worth noting that Ghamaṇḍa Chand who built the fortress at Tira Sujānpur gave his daughter in marriage to Amṛta Pāl of Basohli. The intense red monochrome background is also a feature of this series and which it shares with the *Rasamañjarī* which emerged from the Basohli atelier. This early Kāṅgṛā series also shares some of its bold features with that of the Mankoṭ atelier. The figures are bold and bright and are deployed brilliantly in the architecture.

The Mature Kāṅgṛā Style
8, 11, 15, 16, 17, 21, 23, 25, 26, 29, 30
(National Museum, Delhi)

Sansār Chand who ascended the throne of Kāṅgṛā at the age of 10 in 1776 had a special fondness for romantic paintings and especially that of Kṛṣṇa. On coming of age when he emerged as a paramount power in the Hills and established himself as a great ruler and administrator he turned his attention to the arts and became a connoisseur. At a very young age he had attained political power and success and had developed an impressive atelier in his court. In some of his court paintings he is shown examining paintings with his courtiers. Besides pictorial arts, he was equally interested in romantic poetry, classical music and dance.

Being an epicurean prince Sansār Chand estab-lished a large and active court by extending lavish patronage to painters. His fame as a liberal connoisseur of the arts encouraged several pain-ters from other Hill states and the Plains to join the royal atelier of Kāṅgṛā. One of the painter families that had migrated to Ustehad in the Kāṅgṛā Valley was that of Purkhu who was to become one of the foremost painters at the court of Sansār Chand. This family had earlier migrated from the neighbouring state of Guler. It is problematic to ascribe paintings to Purkhu or his workshop. Since there are no signed works by Purkhu any assessment of his oeuvre has to be done by careful examination and intelligent inference of the pictorial styles and conventions, motifs and designs in Kāṅgṛā paintings of the late eighteenth century. Purkhu was first and foremost an accomplished portrait painter, this was his forte. The many portraits of his patron attest to that. However Purkhu is remembered and celebrated most for his large narrative paintings like those from the *Bhāgavata Purāṇa*, *Harivaṁśa Purāṇa*, *Śiva Purāṇa*, *Pārijātaharaṇa* and *Gīta-Govinda*. Even in these large paintings, populated with so many figures, Purkhu pays attention to each figure and makes it almost a portrait. It is almost certain that either Purkhu or his atelier also produced *citrāvalī*s from Rītīkāvya notably *Rasikapriyā*, *Śatasai* and *Rasarāja*. It is obvious that this amount of artistic output must have required a large atelier where all his sons, collaterals and cousins worked together in the family workshop. Purkhu's style of painting seems to have been influenced by both the Guler and Avadh school of paintings. It would not be wrong to assume that the family of Purkhu, which had migrated from Guler to Kāṅgṛā in first half of the eighteenth century, must have been influenced by pictorial conventions from the Guler Gharānā of the celebrated painter Seu and his illustrious sons. This is seen particularly in the treatment of the landscape and the female figures of Purkhu which carries the characteristic Kāṅgṛā stamp of soft and sensual beauty. However Purkhu also seems to be influenced by Avadh painting when it comes to the multi-tiered and lively architecture that dominate his paintings. Purkhu excelled in painting large-size horizontal *wasli* pasteboards. Typically his compositions are packed by many people in processions or in an ambience of royal grandeur or festive spirit. His signature style are countless figures against monochromatic backgrounds of soft muted colours. In depictions of episodes from the epics like *Rāmāyaṇa, Bhāgavata* or *Harivaṁśa Purāṇa* his compositions are domi-nated by resplendent architectural edifices of glowing marble or golden walls. From *jharokhās* and doors, people in his paintings move in and out. At times the important mythological figures are labelled above their head with brief inscriptions in the Devanāgarī script. Purkhu's figures are never generic, as one sees in his paintings that he has successfully captured the individual facial characteristics of each Pahāṛī chieftain. At times their heads appear somewhat larger than the torsos. A special feature of Purkhu's female figures is this to tender hands with tapering fingers. Most of the male figures seen in his works wear a *jāmā*, a long waistband (*kamarabanda*) and sport a *kuledar* turban, while female figures are shown clad in a *peśawāz* as well as in a *colī* and *ghāgharā*. He prefers to draw one-eyed faces in profile (*ekacaśmī*) rather than one-and-a-half (*deḍha-caśmī*) faces. If the Seu family is the flag-bearer of the Pahāṛī *kalam* Purkhu must be considered the master artist of the atelier of Sansār Chand who along raised Pahāṛī painting to a high art form. When one thinks of the glorious tradition of Kāṅgṛā painting many images pass through the mind's eye: idyllic landscapes, verdant meadows, limpid waters, graceful women with beautiful eyes, splendid architecture, the majesty of royal courts, evocative portraits and with all this the names of Sansār Chand, the extraordinary patron of the arts and Purkhu a master painter will always echo. Both together have left behind a legacy of paintings that will be counted as some of the most beautiful artistic expressions of the late eighteenth and the nineteenth century, where form and feeling, the patron and the painter, regal splendour and tender emotions blend seamlessly into a charmed universe, where Śṛṅgāra Rasa was a *rājā rasa* and the celebration of love in word and image was a cultivated and cherished activity.

Būndī

12, 13 Cover image (Dehejia Collection of Kṛṣṇa Art)

East of Udaipur, the new capital of Mewāṛ, were the twin states of Koṭāh and Būndī (formerly known as Haraoti) which became important sites of Rājpūt painting. The earliest painting from this state is a Cunār Rāgamālā of 1591 but it came into its own in the seventeenth and eighteenth centuries. Rao Chattar Sāl (1631-59) of Būndī was a patron of the arts and the Būndī artistic idiom was characterized by reddish brown flesh tints and an architectural complex featuring open verandas, domed pavilions, manicured gardens, lush plantain trees, water pools, tumultuous skies and with male figures wearing long *jāmās*, narrow *paṭakās* and *cūṛīdāra pyjāmās* and a turban with a broad sash and female figures with narrow waists, women with almond eyes and wearing a *ghāgharā* or *peśawāj*, high *colī* and *oḍhanī* and ornamented by pearls. The Būndī *kalam* was noted for sumptuous luxuriance, a predilection for greens and oranges in juxtaposition, a delight in natural profusion and the use of recessions, shading and round volumes. The Būndī style was lyrical and had refinement, its figures showed grace and there was a certain subdued elegance about its compositions. Būndī had close contacts with the Deccan and Bhao Singh (1658-81) of Būndī was the governor of Auraṅgābād under the last Mughal Bahadur Shah. This contact resulted in a number of Deccani artistic influences in Būndī painting such as patterned floorings, pillared balconies and domed edifices and marked Mughal mannerisms. In the eighteenth century the bright and bold colouring of the Būndī artists was to give way to paler shades and this period is sometimes referred to as the white period of Būndī painting.

Bikaner
1 (Philadelphia Museum of Art)

The wedding scene of Kṛṣṇa and Satyabhāmā is rendered in the typical style of the Bikaner *kalam*. Jāmbavatī and Rukmiṇī, the other two prominent wives of Kṛṣṇa are seen on either side of Satyabhāmā. Rukmiṇī stands on the right with a bowl filled with flower garlands, while Jāmbavatī on the left appears to be proffering an empty bowl, and her mouth is turned decidedly downwards, giving her a rather unhappy appearance. There is a pronounced absence of ornamentation in the clothes of the wedding party. Kṛṣṇa wears a simple, conical headdress typical of the Dvārakā wedding attire, with two gold-centred medallions over each ear. He wears a plain golden *kurtā* tied with a sash, a red *dhotī* or *pyjāmā*, and no jewellery except for a few strands of necklace. Likewise, Satyabhāmā is in a flowing white striped *dupaṭṭā*, with only a bracelet as ornamentation. Both sport sprays of white flowers that sway charmingly above their heads on long, thin stems. It is conceivable that the artist chose to display the divine couple in such an unadorned fashion for he may have wished to emphasize a particular contrast between this unadorned scene and the glittering opulence of the *syamantaka* which resulted in this marriage. The canopy itself is simply ornamented with a *toraṇa* of small oranges and banana leaves. The rectangular block of red featured consistently in many Bikaner paintings is disguised here as the pavilion interior. This *Bhāgavata Purāṇa* series also represents the process by which popular Mughal painting slowly germinated distinctive regional idioms. This series has long been associated with painting at Bikaner, primarily because some of its paintings bear a stamp indicating that they were part of the Bikaner royal collection. The spare compositions, cool palette and pronounced linear quality of this *Bhāgavata Purāṇa* series are akin to those of paintings produced at Bikaner in the last third of the seventeenth century. It is reasonable therefore to see this series as a forerunner of the later Bikaner style. None the less, the Bikaner style seems to have developed in a relatively fitful manner, as is suggested by the thoroughly Mughalized style of a painting inscribed as having been made at Bikaner by the painter Nur Muhammad about the year 1610. The simpler base style and more superficial borrowing of Mughal elements of this *Bhāgavata Purāṇa* series support an earlier date of *c.* 1590–1600, or not long after that of the Isarda *Bhāgavata Purāṇa*.

Nepal
14 (Private Collection)

In the typical Nepali style, the artist presents this episode from *Bhāgavata* with a number of details.

Suvarṇa Tulā
A Play in Marathi

Vidyādhar Gokhale, an accomplished playright, wrote *Suvarṇa Tulā* in the mid-twentieth century. While the first two acts follows the traditional narrative of Pārijātaharaṇa, it is in Act III that Gokhale brilliantly brings in Rādhā to give a closure to the story. Here is an excerpt from Act III.

Champavati: Why do you behave like this? Balarama and Rukmini will arrive shortly.

Friends of Satyabhama (aside): What did you do? You acted out of *dharma* but got into trouble. By donating your husband on account of Narada you made all of us orphans. Who gave you the right to sell your husband alone? You have made all of us widows. How will you pay for your sin?

Satyabhama: I did not intend to do this. What should I do to get out of this trouble?

Chandravati: Rukmini Devi is coming.

Rukmini: Stay calm. We are all responsible for this.

Satyabhama: I will give you my *syamantaka* and *parijata* but please release my husband.

Rukmini: Stop your egoistic behaviour. We better consult an elder like Balarama and Radha.

Satyabhama: Why did you invite Radha? She has brought bad omen to all of Dvaraka.

Rukmini: Radha is not as bad as you think.

Balarama: I will kill Indra for doing this to my brother. How did my brother fall victim to such a scheme? The *parijata* is our banner and we will not return even a leaf of it back to Indra. We will wage war and release Krishna.

Rukmini: Narada has suggested another plan.

Mahamantri: Narada suggests that if Krishna was weighed against gold and the gold is given to Indra then he is prepared to release him.

Satyabhama: That is not a problem. I can easily do it with the help of my *syamantaka* jewel.

Balarama: Get a golden gem-studded weigh scale ready, seeing which Narada will be impressed.

Mahamantri: A downcast looking Krishna following Narada is coming towards us.

Narada: Go and sit in the corner and not on the throne. Krishna is my servant. Organize the scales and let us proceed with the weighing.

Krishna go and sit on the right side of the scale.

Balarama: Treasurer! Put all the gold coins on the other side.

Treasurer: We have put 5 maunds of gold but yet the scales do not trip.

Balarama: Go and get my personal gold coins and put it on the scale.

Treasurer: The treasury is empty but yet we cannot tip the scales.

Balarama: Place all the personal treasures of Rukmini, Satyabhama and all the wives on the scale.

Treasurer: Even after all that the scales do not move.

Balarama: Place my golden crown in it.

Narada: Just drop it. Not all the jewels of Dvaraka will tip the scales. Instead let Krishna be my servant. Why this show of love towards Krishna?

Balarama: There seems to be some black magic here.

Satyabhama: Do not worry. Let me place my *syamantaka* jewel in the scale.

Balarama: Yes, please do that. It will show the strength of your love.

Champavati: Maharaja! Someone called Radha has come here.

Balarama: Send her in immediately and set Krishna free.

Radha: How can Krishna, who frees everyone from the bondage of this *samsara*, be captured? One who is always in our *atman*, how can he escape?

Satyabhama: We have lost all our gold and treasures but we have not been able to release Krishna.

Radha: Devotees of Hari never give up hope. The scales will tilt. Let us put real gold in that.

Satyabhama: So is what we have placed brass!

Krishna: Radha please release me from this.

Narada: Please hand over Krishna to me.

Rukmini: We have exhausted our gold but we still have precious stones.

Radha: Even if you put the entire coffer of Kubera it will not suffice. You are all groping in the dark. You will have to put a different kind of treasure.

Rukmini: Where is that treasure? Go and get it.

Radha: It is right here in the treasure of your heart. Just as the musk deer forgets the source of the aroma and the lotus does not remember the honey within it, how can you forget your treasure? Know yourself for you are none other than the *shakti* of Krishna.

Narada: Radha enough of your lecture. Place whatever treasure you have.

Radha: We all have that treasure more precious than gold and jewels. If I have loved Krishna truly and if my love is as pure as Ganga and if every part of my body is Krishnamaya then let me find that treasure that will release Krishna.

Rukmini: Radha I have found the treasure that you are talking about.

Radha: Yes, if you have found that treasure then place this *tulsi* leaf on the scale.

Rukmini: Champavati! Go and get a *tulsi* leaf.

Rukmini goes towards the scale chanting the praise of Krishna and placed the *tulsi* leaf. The scales tip.

Balarama: Victory to Radha.